THE
HIGH
GROWTH
NON
PROFIT

MATT SCOTT

THE
HIGH
GROWTH
NON
PROFIT

PROVEN STEPS TO QUICKLY
DOUBLE YOUR REVENUE
AND DRIVE IMPACT

To request permission, contact matt@causemic.com

ISBN 979-8-218-15613-8
Printed in the United States of America
First edition

Edited by Drew Lewis, Paddy O'Neill, and Craig Seligman
Cover & layout design by Chris Frees

Published by CauseMic
2034 N Killingsworth St, Portland, OR 97217
causemic.com

To Madelyn and all the future idealists.

CONTENTS

PREFACE

BUT, WHY NOT?

Get to "Yes."

The words appeared clearly in my mind. A directive I once received that I would later pass along to the team at our Hot Start, an action-oriented all-staff we hold twice a year.

I was staring at our One Page Strategic Plan on the heels of another year of fast growth. Our nonprofit growth consultancy did it again. *CauseMic* grew revenue by 62.5%, exceeding our target by nearly 10%. We achieved most of what we sought at the beginning of last year. We also eliminated single points of failure through a combination of hiring and frameworks. Nonetheless, like so much of our growth, it felt more like a starting line than a mission accomplished. There was much more to do.

CauseMic exists to fully fund every nonprofit that aligns with our values of building a more just and equitable world. We do this by empowering leaders of mission-driven organizations to quickly grow their revenue in order to scale their impact. No money, no mission. As nonprofit leaders, we all know that. So when the time came to review our own marketing plan, I was convinced that one way we could deliver value to you was by passing on lessons learned from helping hundreds of nonprofit leaders scale their organizations. Enter this book.

There was only one problem, one that we're all too familiar with. There was more to do than time to do it. I was working with an aggressive timeline. I told my trusted thought partner, Bobbi, that I wanted the book completed in 90 days. She turns so many of my ideas into outcomes—I start things, she finishes them. It's a beautiful partnership that energizes me and delivers value to you. Bobbi knew this lofty target was beyond ambitious. I'm no Stephen King. I've never written a book, so what made me think that I could turn a prolific author's 20-week process into a mere 12? Naivete, sure. But, also the mandate: *Get to "Yes."*

As you'll gather in the chapters ahead, I live for the Kennedy moonshot. Now, is a book authored in 90 days as ambitious as a nation sending a person to the moon by the end of the decade? Probably not, unless you think of it in terms of available resources. You're right—still not. Nonetheless, for me to quickly capture for you the many lessons that I've learned in a meaningful way was my own moonshot.

Bottom Line

I missed the deadline.

Bobbi was right. My timeline was a tad lofty by almost half. It took 152 (not 90) days to detail the most valuable lessons I've learned over ten years, whether helping to scale nonprofits from within or as a consultant. Throughout the book, I've tried to keep in mind how limited and valuable your time is. That's why I've avoided "burying the lead" by putting key takeaways up front in each chapter. If you come across one of these and find yourself yelling, "Bullshit!" I encourage you to read that chapter. I cover not just what to do, but how to do it.

So, let's get to it. Your accelerated growth starts here.

01

OUTGROW THAT 5% MINDSET

BOILING IT DOWN TO TWO

The first step in growing your nonprofit is reframing your mindset from modest incremental increases to exponential possibilities that invite bold growth spurts.

Liberate your growth by taking risks to capture limited donor dollars; don't squander donation opportunities by setting a goal well below what your team is capable of fundraising.

It's January when your nonprofit team shuffles back into the office, refreshed and perhaps a few pounds heavier from too many holiday dinners and desserts. With hot cups of coffee in hand, people take their seats around the conference table to start the year's first planning and strategy meeting. Your team goes over results from the year-end fundraising campaign, which everyone agrees was good but not great.

Next order of business is a sweeping rundown of programs and operations, bookended with key goals for increasing the organization's impact. This is when *you* bravely propose a bold idea—gathering the room's attention in the process—that reframes the team's mindset around growth. You ask: **"What if we had no choice but to double our revenue over the next three years with half the resources, half the human effort, half the budget? How would we do it?** *Go.***"**

And you're met with blank looks and deafening silence.

Trust me, it takes a minute for people to grasp, because it sounds like a hypothetical question. It's not. Well, no one is really halving your resources, so that part kind of is. However, it's real in the sense that doubling revenue (or better!) does *not* require doubling or even maxing out resources. Let's face it—you could buy a high-end stationary bike that rhymes with *Shmeloton*, or you could get the same great workout on a cheaper one without some video person shaming you.

Reframing your organization's growth mindset is the first step in doubling your nonprofit's revenue in three years or less.

And yes, it's absolutely possible.

My career began in nonprofits where I cut my teeth as a fundraiser learning how to reach new donors. I listened and tried new things, and soon enough I was leading my own fundraising team at an organization called *Team Rubicon* that specializes in veteran-led disaster response.

During my seven years there, we took the organization from $275,000 in annual revenue to $51 million.

Team Rubicon grew in rapid spurts with more than just luck (which is nice to have). We grew by reframing how we thought about growth from *incremental* ("The organization is targeting a five percent increase in revenue this year") to *significant* ("Let's double, scratch that, *triple* what we raised last year").

Bold thinking invites bold ideas. Bold ideas generate bold results.

After more than a decade as a nonprofit growth consultant, I've found it's actually the larger, more established nonprofits that are reluctant to think beyond incremental growth. It's not hard to understand why—they have more to lose and they have more stakeholders to align. This was the case for one of our consultancy's long-time clients: an international aid organization with thousands of employees and chapters in dozens of countries.

It wasn't until the day they asked us, "How do we increase annual revenue by five percent?" that I realized their plateaued growth wasn't because of how they operated or some broken process. They were seeing smaller, year-over-year increases because that's where they'd consistently set the bar! And of course they'd reach it, which is fine. But why settle for low-hanging fruit when you could be munching on higher-up sun-drenched beauties?

Plus, it doesn't do any good if your operational goals are outpacing available revenue streams. You're forced to either cut back or constrain your services and programs, limiting the good you can do for clients and community.

So, at the risk of being rude, I answered their five-percent question with a question:

What if instead you aim to double your revenue over the next three years with half the resources?

Ring a bell?

Long story short, they agreed to a bold strategy, inherent risks and all, and it paid off big. In fact, they grew their net new revenue by 87% in just one year! Had they not taken a bold leap, an ominous possibility could have become a reality. This well-positioned, international nonprofit may well have relinquished *market share* to smaller organizations willing to throw caution to the wind for meteoric growth.

HOLD THE PHONE—DID HE SAY "MARKET SHARE?" QUITE SO, FOR TWO REASONS:

01. There is only so much donation money available in total, regardless of which "cause arena" (or, nonprofit sector) you're in. Donors decide which of these are important to them and act accordingly, splintering this already finite pot of money into all of the nonprofit sectors.

02. This now choked-down donor funding gets redistributed even further into all of the nonprofits operating in the same sector. If a donor wants to make a bigger impact for a certain cause, say animal welfare, they might look into a number of those nonprofits, but most likely will *pick one* that allows them to do the most good with their hard-earned money.

First of all, should your overall cause attract donations? Of course. Are you *THE* nonprofit in your cause arena that's most deserving of hard-earned donor money? Again, yes, right? This is competition, and thus you vie for market share.

I have a strong suspicion that you hold a leadership position in a mid-to-large sized nonprofit. Someone that has the authority to decide things, like President/CEO, Executive Director, perhaps another in the C-Suite?

Or, maybe you're a Director of Fundraising, Marketing, or even HR!

Whichever your management role, you're likely reading this because you want to grow your organization, your team, your revenue, and most importantly, your impact.

And you can do that by tapping into the hearts and minds of current and potential supporters.

02

I QUIT THINKING LIKE A TRADITIONAL NONPROFIT AND NEVER LOOKED BACK

BOILING IT DOWN TO TWO

Ditch the status quo, and give your organization the room and tools it needs to stay relevant. Whisk your nonprofit into its next phase of growth, but never forget the personal touch.

Look beyond what your nonprofit peers are doing, and borrow industry-leading examples from for-profits. Who says what they're doing isn't relevant?!

I'll never forget the one decision I made that initially pissed off some folks.

It was 2012, and *Team Rubicon* was a spry, two-year-old nonprofit. "Think at scale" was the mandate. I was at the helm of our fundraising team and decided to dive in and purchase *Salesforce*, the organization's first customer relationship management (CRM) subscription.

I made the big-budget move because I knew it would be crucial for *Team Rubicon* to continue growing, and not everyone was happy about it. Come on, it's not like we had official department budgets. Did we even have department budgets? I don't remember having a department budget.

We were moving at lightning speed, and my decision was made in calculated haste and in somewhat of a silo. Yep, I likely should've consulted or informed a few more stakeholders about their requirements and the platform's possibilities, but at that stage of growth, I don't have a single regret about the investment.

What prompted this CRM decision was our response to Superstorm Sandy, a truly catastrophic disaster. We had hundreds of volunteers on the ground in New York and donations pouring in from across the country. Rather than an expensive risk, I saw a CRM as our only choice. To not capitalize on all the new donors we'd welcomed into our mission would be to fail communities devastated by future disasters.

In the end, the Co-Founder and CEO at the time, Jake Wood, was very supportive of my decision to purchase an industry-leading CRM. After all, I was following the North Star he'd set for *Team Rubicon*. (More on your North Star in Chapter Four.)

My vindication aside, before then, we didn't have a great way to welcome new donors to our mission. So one day soon after the storm, I sat down at my desk, picked up the phone, and personally began calling hundreds of donors. I then hand-wrote them letters. Anyone who gave, regardless of amount, received a call and a note thanking them for their generosity.

It seemed to take forever. But you know what?

People were blown away.

In fact, some were so blown away that they remained monthly donors ten years later after I'd already left the organization. Their stated reason in part for continued giving was the call, letter, or both they received from us.

It's a cool enough story, something I'm proud of earlier in my career. But here's the thing (if you haven't already guessed): *it's not sustainable.*

It was incredibly tiring and a questionable use of time and budget. That's why I purchased *Salesforce.* I'd already been hearing how CRMs were becoming the standard at for-profit companies, and believed they should be at nonprofits, too.

That same year, I attended a *Salesforce* conference called *Dreamforce* in San Francisco. I got the meat and potatoes of how companies were using *Salesforce* to build better relationships with their customers and to boost revenue, which is what I wanted to do with donors. Perfect. Then on my flight home, I read an article about a company called *Chewy* that grabbed 40 percent of the online market share of pet supplies in one year.

How *Chewy* did it was through highly personalized engagements with customers.

They sent hand-written notes to new customers. For those whose pets had passed away, *Chewy* sent flowers. They commissioned portraits of randomly selected pets whose photos appeared on their *Chewy* account. And they mailed each and every customer a holiday card.

It got me thinking.

I'd discovered the value in highly personalized outreach myself, and now I saw the bigger picture, the full potential!

Imagine how we could grow *Team Rubicon's* donor base by combining technology with extreme personalization. It was a true *Aha!* moment for me, one that I'm sure was audibly displeasing to passengers and crew.

First, we worked with *Classy* and *Salesforce* developers to marry both systems into an effective, streamlined donor-based technology.

We then used photojournalists to provide current, compelling content. And we adopted a multi-channel approach that incorporated personalized messaging to foster a rich donor experience.

In a year, we increased revenue by 219%, from $3.2M to $7M.

Fast forward from 2013, those principles hold true today. And at *CauseMic*, we're constantly helping new clients implement best-in-class, *for-profit* technology and leverage it to scale donor personalization.

The result? We help them double their revenue.

03

SO MUCH TO DO, SO LITTLE CAPACITY

BOILING IT DOWN TO TWO

Nonprofits operate in resource-constrained environments, and it's normal to feel you have no capacity for anything other than daily tasks.

Identifying your three top-level priorities and ensuring they're understood is the first step in steering your talent, resources, and mission forward.

There's that cliche movie scene where they're introducing a family and show a mother holding a baby, making breakfast, shoving bag lunches into backpacks as her kids run out the door, all while she's trying to get ready for work, and the husband is casually sipping his coffee. You've seen something like this, yes?

Most nonprofit leaders, if not all, can identify with this go-getter in their daily responsibilities running a growing organization—the laid-back husband with his coffee, not so much.

But even this supermom juggling ten things at once eventually runs into capacity constraints. There's only time to manage must-do's with no time for anything else. Most nonprofit teams likewise become quickly overwhelmed. My team and I at *CauseMic* know this firsthand, having come from high-growth nonprofits.

You probably have a document saved somewhere. A list of great ideas to propel your mission forward, but you and your team can't get to it without putting off critical day-to-day tasks. I've got plenty lying around—but with the prioritization strategies I'll be sharing throughout this book, we're actually able to put lots of checks in boxes.

How, you may ask? By unlocking our team's true capacity.

WHAT I'VE LEARNED HELPING NONPROFITS UNLOCK THEIRS

The biggest lesson I've learned is a 30,000-foot observation that's so simple and yet the key to finding solutions. It's a two-parter:

01. Most teams can only focus on at most three organizational objectives or initiatives at one time while
maintaining efficiency.

02. Leadership must clearly state and reaffirm what
those three priorities *are*.

There are *formal* ways you can do this. An example is a
one-page strategic plan (OPSP), a well thought-out and concise
document breaking down what your organization plans to accomplish within a certain timeframe. Take a look:

Because an OPSP takes time and often requires collaboration
with key stakeholders, it's perfectly fine in the interim to discuss and agree upon three organizational priorities and get the
show on the road. The *informal* route, if you will.

Next, it's critical when everyone is using the same framework to categorize priorities, such as how you define "Priority 1" (P.1), P.2, P.3, and so on.

Our friends at *Thorn*, an organization building technology to defend children from sexual abuse, was growing and moving fast and facing capacity constraints. My team and I introduced them to a framework we created that groups priorities by *level of impact* and *level of effort* required.

This model is meant for top mission priorities and the work needed to get there. It looks like this:

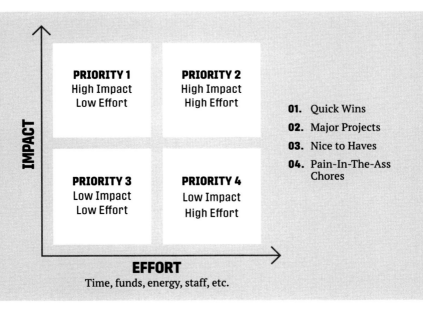

As a starting reference point, this "project backlog" has been a game-changer when beginning our collaborative work with *Thorn* and other clients. Of course, everything from projects to Key Performance Indicators (KPIs) have to be closely tracked as well, which I'll go into a bit later.

Nonprofits will always operate in resource-constrained environments, seemingly unable to move past daily operations and into growth-spurring endeavors. So please don't feel like the Lone Ranger. But throughout these chapters, I'll show you how you can add capacity with the resources you have by channeling your talent and budget into shared goals and one incredible mission.

Repeat after me: "I'm not alone!"

04

YOUR NORTH STAR— SHOWING THE WAY TO AN ULTIMATE GOAL

BOILING IT DOWN TO TWO

Nonprofit leaders should adopt the North Star as a guiding light for the organization's direction, ensuring all team members know what it is and that it drives management decisions toward an ultimate vision.

The North Star is unique to the organization and differs from the mission statement. Unlike the latter offering what the organization does and how it does it, the North Star is a statement that declares *why* in the form of an inspirational goal.

As the story for kids used to go, if you get lost, just look into the night sky and find the North Star to guide you home. That never really made much sense, because lost kids have no idea where their house is. But when it comes to nonprofits charting the best course for their cause, I'm all in.

What exactly is a North Star? Simply put, it's your ambition, your vision. It's the whole point of being in business in the first place; it's more about *why* than *what*.

The North Star's ultimate purpose is to light your way toward even seemingly impossible horizons.

Let's say your North Star is to end hunger in your community. And then a lucrative grant opportunity arises to provide job training to the unemployed. Do you pursue it? Your North Star says "no," because working the grant would strip vital resources from your mission of providing food.

The North Star serves as a filter against which every big decision made by your team is tested. It's incredibly valuable, because it asks of you: Is this really part of our mission? It should be known and spoken of often as a reminder from the organization's leaders. By pointing to your organization's North Star, you give your team permission to stretch, to innovate, to do what it takes to reach even the most ambitious goal.

Co-founders Jake Wood and William McNulty told us their expectation for *Team Rubicon* was to *become the best disaster response organization in the world*. They didn't dare say that we *were* the best disaster response organization in the world at the time; nor would anyone else. It was arguably pretty lofty stuff.

But it became our North Star.

What this ultimately gave me as a leader of the fundraising team was the confidence to make bold decisions on behalf of the organization. It told me that taking risks was not only okay, but downright necessary. (Again, I proudly stand by my previously noted *Salesforce* decision.)

Certainly, the first handful of years saw *Team Rubicon* well south of their vision. Here's a quick story of our impossible dream uniting and guiding us when it mattered, when things got scary.

It was 2017, and as meteorologists had predicted, Hurricane Harvey crashed into the greater Houston area with catastrophic results. It had been five years since our response to Superstorm Sandy, and no one on the team was certain we were ready to respond at the scale expected by emergency managers, donors, volunteers, and people around the country. But each of us was ready to give it all we had and put our CEO on national news asking for funding and volunteers.

Could we handle the influx of donations, of people signing up to go from all 50 states, Canada, and Puerto Rico? This was the overarching question. But according to our North Star, the obvious answer was, "How can we not?" And that was that.

To this day, the response in Houston is still considered among *Team Rubicon's* most memorable and impactful operations. We mobilized thousands of volunteers to serve nearly as many homeowners. And it led to exponential growth in both revenue and volunteers.

My time with the organization taught me many lessons, and the importance of calling out the North Star is one I've held onto quite tightly.

I should note the difference between your North Star and your mission statement. The North Star is essentially your inspirational vision—a kind of *why* you're in business. Your mission statement declares *what* the nonprofit does and usually *how* it does it. Back to our previous example, your North Star may be to end hunger in your community. Your *mission*, however, is to provide food to underserved neighborhoods on a regular basis.

Think of your North Star as the reasoning that prompted you to found your nonprofit in the first place or that convinced you to join the team. Maybe that North Star is the dream that no dog is ever left in a shelter, or as our friends at client *DigDeep* note,

"We believe that every American has a right to clean, running water."

DigDeep takes their North Star quite seriously, because, sadly, not every American has access to clean drinking water and they aim to change that. It's the mentality behind every new program they launch, their ongoing commitment to the Navajo Nation where they began, and why they've expanded to help get clean, reliable drinking water to those in the Appalachian region.

CauseMic's North Star is to fully fund every nonprofit organization. What's yours? What guides you, your staff, and volunteers toward your inspired vision?

05

CULTURE IS THE GLUE

BOILING IT DOWN TO TWO

Work with your team to distill into short and sweet statements what makes your culture unique and powerful. Worry less about the cool phrases at first, and center on the values that matter most to your team and mission. The best cultures often arise from memories already made together.

Having organizational culture creates a sense of oneness through shared values, provides a baseline for problem-solving, and keeps everyone on track when the going gets tough.

Oh wow. You're considering skipping this chapter, brushing off cultural principles as "nice to have, but not something we need right now." You may want to put a pin in that. Every organization needs to create a recognizable, lasting culture. As a leader, it's your responsibility to define, nurture, and protect it. No matter your stage of growth.

Nonprofit teams are arguably lean, and their leaders are not always available to make smaller decisions while flying the plane at 30,000 feet. When the tempo picks up, solutions can be found by any staff member in the last place you might think to look: In the team's cultural principles.

These principles are there to help solve problems, fill in the blanks, and keep everyone on the same track. They're more than a flashy section on your website or a poster on the conference room wall. They're a fundamental part of your growth strategy.

I'll explain what culture does for us at *CauseMic*, as well as what it's like to experience a strong organizational culture in action during a disaster.

But first: How do we define cultural principles?

I'd call them a concisely worded list of agreed-upon values that bind a team together, guiding the actions and decisions of every stakeholder. And they should be representative of everyone on the team at the time chisel first meets stone.

Early in my career, I'd heard of this idea about company culture mentioned nonchalantly, but it wasn't until I landed at *Team Rubicon* that I saw the light, so to speak. Leader Jake Wood was like a broken record with, "In the absence of a defined direction, your organization's culture and values kick in."

And holy shit, did he mean it.

In those days, circa 2011, *Team Rubicon* was running purely on empathy and the organization's cultural principles. Donations were reliable but limited. After major disasters, nearly every staff member was out there alongside volunteers, digging out mud from a family's home or removing a fallen tree from their roof. It's what you did. Our cultural principles shined the way, and they're a big reason any of us were there to begin with.

A COUPLE OF EXAMPLES:

- **"Mission first, Greyshirts Always."** (Greyshirts = *Team Rubicon* volunteers.) Even employees are disaster response volunteers if so needed.
- **"Your mother is a donor."** For any mission to have an impact requires spending big bucks. It's important to remember those bucks are hard-earned and generously gifted by donors like your own momma, so spend responsibly but invest boldly. *Fly coach, so you can bet on Salesforce.*
- **"Get shit done (GSD)."** Number one on the hit parade. It's even been spotted as a tattoo a time or two.

NOW AT CAUSEMIC, WE'VE GOT SOME GOOD ONES TOO:

- **"Sleeves up."** We're builders and doers. We can talk high-level strategies and get down to brass tacks. No one is too good or over-qualified to tackle the dirty work. In fact, we thrive in the execution phase of any project just as much as we love brainwriting (it's a thing) about big ideas.
- **"Success is not final."** Winston Churchill wrote, "Success is not final, failure is not fatal: it is the courage to continue that counts." We celebrate the wins and reflect on the misses, but we're always thinking about our next best move on behalf of the nonprofits we serve—whether tried and true methods or a *Hail Mary* for the win.

- **"The future belongs to the curious."** Defined and fostered in the digital age, *CauseMic's* affinity for innovation remains steadfast. We save the good ol' days banter for high school reunions and work to blaze trails with new technologies and techniques on behalf of our clients' missions. In sum, we challenge, "Is there a better way?"
- **"Show, don't tell."** We're about proof and inspiring our nonprofit clients with results they can see firsthand. Ultimately, we let our revenue-generating work do the talking.
- **"Make time fly."** If time flies when you're having fun, we lost track of it in 2014 when *CauseMic* was established. A work day (and life) is too short to dwell on the obstacles, so we choose to focus on the opportunities, build an alternative path, and probably laugh a tad too much while we're at it.

A way to test the strength of your organization's culture is being able to point to stories of it in action. Making it through the pandemic comes to mind for me. In what felt like an instant, *CauseMic* lost 65% of its forecasted work when the pandemic pushed humanity (and business) into survival mode.

Like everyone, we were scared. The team went home, rolled up our collective sleeves (pajamas have sleeves) and started making calls to see who and how we could help.

One of those calls was with *Greater Good Charities (GGC)*, who needed a technology solution ASAP to save tens of thousands of animals after shelter workers were told to stay home. Why a technology solution? GGC had a quick plan called "Stay Home and Foster," but they needed a holistic systems overhaul to connect potential foster-pet parents with the shelters. We ran a four-day sprint to fully implement a new CRM with the required integrations. Our work helped GGC recruit and connect 96,000 volunteer pet fosters with a little under 5,000 shelters nationwide. If that's not a sleeves-up moment, I'm not sure what is.

○ ○ ○

So... how do you come up with cool-sounding cultural phrases?

An advantage for a nonprofit doing this for the first time is that your team is likely a smaller number of folks who probably know each other fairly well. On the other hand, an established nonprofit also has an advantage, in that more team members can contribute and how the organization operates is more evident.

There's no formula for defining your nonprofit's principles, and that's a good thing. It gives you and your team the freedom to write your own script. Narrowing down the long list of values associated with your mission and, more importantly, the good people driving it is done with feeling and self-reflection, which will hopefully surface the values shared among the team.

Now start asking questions to dig out initial information. For example, does the team have a unique working style? Are fast and ugly presentations favored over prettier slides that take a week to create? Is the team up before the sun or burning midnight oil? Is working weekends off-limits (the work-life balance notion)?

Once you're done with the more low-hanging fruit, you can mine deeper, perhaps even create an internal survey. My advice—don't worry about the phrase or definition at first. Nail down the values (and quirks!) that matter most to the team. Then, later on you can give it a nice coat of paint. Your organization has an identity, so be unique and inclusive and whatever you land on will be golden.

06

KEEP KNOWING TO KEEP GROWING

BOILING IT DOWN TO TWO

It's vitally important as a leader to understand which phase of growth your nonprofit is in; you'll then know the next crisis to come and how to handle it.

Don't reuse solutions for previous crises or try to skip phases; doing either jeopardizes future growth and success.

In a classic 1972 article from the *Harvard Business Review*, Larry Greiner talks about the five phases of growth a for-profit company will go through on its way to reaching maturity. At the time when I first read "Evolution and Revolution as Organizations Grow," I was leading a fundraising team. I read it often, actually. It really resonated. I couldn't get over how applicable it was for nonprofits, even though it was written decades ago with for-profit companies in mind.

As I read and reread Greiner's essay, I switched out core functions, such as substituting *Donations and Fundraising* for *Sales*. This gave the essay a more relevant nonprofit slant as it laid out crises and solutions involved with phases of growth.

Of course, there was more to consider beyond switching out a few key terms—how each original phase would apply chronologically to any nonprofit, for example.

We're only going to scratch the surface here, because there's a lot to be said. But if this really has you intrigued—and I hope it does—head to *CauseMic.com/blog* and read my in-depth explanation under: "*Phases of Growth and Crisis in the Life of Nonprofits.*" I'm sure you'll recognize the phase you're in, and then see what lies ahead.

Okay. So Greiner's "Evolution" and "Revolution" terms refer to a period of growth and the turmoil following it, respectively.

Essentially, Evolutions are times when things are going swimmingly, and no major upheaval occurs in organizational practices—until it all starts slipping. Enter a Revolution. Revolutions are times of crisis that naturally result from periods of high growth. This is because solutions that lead your nonprofit into new growth will inevitably breed problems that can cause it to fail. And what fixes *that* problem ultimately ushers in another Revolution, and so on.

Nonprofits that reach maturity and unlimited potential will go through five phases of growth (meaning, five phases of Evolutions and Revolutions). That's not to say your organization will move through each phase at the same pace as any other organization, because everyone's circumstances are likely somewhat unique.

One thing I always tell nonprofit leaders to keep in mind is the importance of identifying where your team is in the grand sequence.

I'll say that again. **Knowing which phase you're in is critical for sustained growth.** Organizations that know what they'll face next and how to prepare for it will likely continue to thrive.

It's also important to note that retreads of solutions to earlier crises are ineffective, as employing them would make it virtually impossible for new growth to occur. And skipping phases eliminates the experience of what works and doesn't work. In short, each evolution and revolution builds needed strengths for future success.

Can you recognize your current phase and whether you're experiencing an Evolution or Revolution?

PHASE 1

Evolution: **Growth through Origins**
You've come up with a bold idea to make a difference in the world and founded a nonprofit with limitless potential. Soon enough, success leads to infrastructure requirements and management responsibilities that few entrepreneurial founders wish to take on.

Thus a Revolution: **Crisis of Leadership**
A good leader, most often a CEO, is either brought on or appointed (let's call that person "you"). You then (1) build a formal management team, (2) create processes and expectations, and (3) lead the nonprofit organization out of this crisis.

PHASE 2

Evolution: **Growth through Directive Leadership**
You're an executive leading and keeping the team focused through one-way, unshared directive action. The organization is growing, broadening programs to meet greater needs, developing strong strategies to scale, and establishing formal hierarchies and communication policies. Eventually, however, this top-down decision-making hits a wall.

Thus a Revolution: **Crisis of Autonomy**
The nonprofit has grown, becoming more complex and impersonal. Mid- to lower-level managers complain their hands are tied by executive orders, and they're feeling unempowered to make the decisions they believe necessary to do their jobs well. In short, they lack autonomy.

PHASE 3

Evolution: **Growth through Delegation**
You recognize your program teams are experts in what they do and are in the best position to know their job needs. You shift to management by delegation, giving greater responsibility to now-motivated managers who can make their own tactical decisions. By now, your nonprofit is well-established with varied funding streams, and things are great. Until you and your senior leadership team feel a loss of control.

Thus a Revolution: **Crisis of Control**
Top management feels it's losing control of the nonprofit's diverse, autonomously run operations. Program and department managers are resistant to yielding control they've been given, creating a paralyzing stalemate across the organization that also causes it to lose touch with its clients.

The nonprofit is now too big to return to directive leadership. The organization is likely on its way out, unless some sort of organizational coordination is put in place.

PHASE 4

Evolution: **Growth through Coordination**
You and your leadership team implement formal systems designed to foster coordination across departments, and everyone is made aware that they are expected to participate. While a measure of autonomy is still in place, managers must now justify decisions to administrative staff. As such, the nonprofit climbs another rung, but finds its next snag with a sign reading: Approval Needed.

Thus a Revolution: **Crisis of Red Tape**
Program teams "on the ground" resent rigid requirements and administrative staff who know little about operations, and staff resents uncooperative program managers. Red tape is at every turn, and organizational bureaucracy now favors procedure over problem-solving. Goodbye innovation, and hello impasse. Unless collaboration is put into play, there's nowhere to go but down.

PHASE 5

Evolution: **Growth through Collaboration**
Leadership opens wider channels of communication that embrace conversation over approval. More managers are invited to speak in cross-departmental meetings, propelling quick problem-solving and cutting through the red tape. A real appreciation develops for the people driving the mission, along with encouragement of

innovation and behavior skill training. Additionally, self-discipline and social control replace formality, and frequent meetings replace resentment. Collaboration abounds.

And the Revolution?
This is basically the end of Greiner's road. Where widespread collaboration leads is unknown. He believes it may simply be exhaustion from both continuous teamwork and the pressure for innovation. At this point, the nonprofit is essentially peaking in its scalable growth and whatever the crisis to emerge might be, revitalization is key.

EXAMPLES OF NONPROFIT CLIENTS DRIVING TO THE NEXT PHASE

01. Our friends at *World Bicycle Relief* (WBR) grew from an entrepreneurial start-up to a global organization with worldwide revenue streams. Rapidly expanding, they eventually encountered a *Crisis of Autonomy* and recognized their need to empower on-the-ground directors to make decisions. Granting greater permissions to teams running their programs with less oversight from headquarters made it possible to quickly extend their outreach to a fast-growing supporter base. As such, they ushered WBR into its next phase: Growth through Delegation.

02. The *Surfrider Foundation* has been around for decades and boasts over 85 chapters nationwide. Though they had a substantial amount of brand recognition, *Surfrider Foundation* hit fundraising and volunteer-engagement snags due to decentralized technology platforms. Essentially, they found themselves in a Crisis of Control. Embracing Growth through Coordination, they moved all chapters to

centralized systems, enabling them to fully understand the volunteer and supporter life cycles which
had become fragmented and duplicative.

So—now armed with Greiner's Evolution and Revolution
knowledge, did you identify your nonprofit's current growth or
crisis phase? And are you prepared for what comes next?

07

TAKING A JACKHAMMER TO THAT CONCRETE PLAN

BOILING IT DOWN TO TWO

A plan is only as good as its ability to adapt.

An effective North Star gives you the courage to make bold moves for notable growth.

I'm a strong believer that a plan is a great place to deviate from because, frankly, you can't plan for everything. As noted in a 1957 speech by President Eisenhower, "Plans are worthless, but planning is everything."

Nearly all nonprofits operate in fluid environments where a sudden spike in the needs of communities are common. Unpredictable weather bringing disaster to a small town. Homelessness worsened by economic turmoil. Protected land and wildlife at risk from an abrupt legislation change. Not to mention fundraising being heavily swayed by a trending news story.

Having a strong, well-thought-out plan for the year or multiple years, depending on which phase of growth you're in, is critical. It's also critical to have adaptable strategies that enable the team to change course when life gives you lemons. Maybe it's a new fundraising opportunity and you turn those proverbial lemons into lemonade. Or, it's a sudden need to adapt out of necessity. Either way, an organization built to adapt is built to succeed.

The destination should remain the same. Guided by your North Star, having to detour from your planned route is simply another way to pursue your ultimate goal.

I have an excellent example from our work with a great organization called the *Selamta Family Project* (SFP) that provides forever families, homes, and services for orphaned or abandoned children in Ethiopia.

They first came to us with the million-dollar question: How do we raise more money for our mission?

Running programs in Ethiopia has added challenges due to poverty along with political and economic turmoil. But SFP refused to let it halt their urgent mission and wrap-around care for these children of all ages who would otherwise have little hope for stability.

Here was this growing organization guided by its North Star ("Every child deserves the love of a family"), needing to increase revenue quickly if they were going to create their desired impact.

SFP had a great five-year plan. It was made stronger by their willingness to adapt, which really came into play when they learned of a specific U.S. audience drawn to what they were doing—faith-based donors.

Though SFP's core message had always had a religious tilt, they had long kept it mostly internal for fear of alienating a more secular donor base. However, leadership decided to broadcast their faith loud and clear for their fundraising efforts, providing potential donors a closer look at their organization.

People with strong religious beliefs tend to be family oriented. As such, along with SFP uniting orphaned children with family units instead of an orphanage, airing their religious platform resonated loudly with U.S. faith-based groups.

In essence, their North Star guided them to take a chance, to embrace a bold risk, because providing children with a loving home life is everything.

And bold is good, right?

It certainly was for SFP and the impact they were able to make by adjusting their plan to reach this important (and generous) demographic. They didn't suddenly become a religious organization, which could have come off as inauthentic. Rather, they used genuine and true-to-themselves information to guide their campaign strategies.

It was an absolutely exciting time to be partnering with SFP, that's for sure!

CauseMic had the opportunity to help connect them with religious organizations in the U.S., putting their mission front and center of those who would likely care the most.

FOLLOWING THEIR ADAPTIVE NEW FUNDRAISING STRATEGY, WE:

- Rebranded their monthly giving program
- Sent a team to help shoot a video with a high-profile corporate partner
- Launched a successful peer-to-peer fundraising campaign
- Helped them expand inspirational storytelling online
- And in doing so, helped them double their campaign revenue on multiple occasions

Perhaps an even better way to interpret a deviation from a set plan is the same plan evolving to do more good.

08

THE VALUE OF BEING DECISIVE, INCLUSIVE, AND IMPERFECT

BOILING IT DOWN TO TWO

No leader is perfect. But by being decisive, celebrating wins, sharing misses, and learning from mistakes, you'll get closer than most!

Resist the urge to follow another nonprofit's approach just because they're doing something you're not. Follow your own path, grow at your own speed, and lead your team.

By this point in the book, you should know that I'm in your corner on growing your nonprofit mission. Whether you're a Founder, CEO, Director, or Manager, title aside—you believe in what you're building and so do I.

We put a lot of pressure on ourselves. Being in a leadership position can lead to compounding anxiety—real or imagined— of the need to be perfect. I'm sure a lot of that is just me being too hard on myself.

But I'm also optimistic by nature, and at the risk of sounding like a school counselor, that's basically what this chapter is about.

Celebrate your wins! Remember to cheer for your successes like you just ended world hunger—hyperbole aside, this is important. Every win, big or small, moves your mission ahead; so take a moment with your team to celebrate it. They made it happen, and there's nothing like feeling appreciated to make your people stick around.

You're not perfect, and that's a good thing (nobody likes a showoff). There's really no greater way to learn what doesn't work than to try it and fall short. That just means your next effort has a better chance of hitting the mark. Even if you make mistakes with donor dollars, the learning process will breed solutions for longer-term stability, because you're committed to not repeating those mistakes.

The real secret here for organizational growth is not how close to flawless you can get, but how decisive you are. A naval officer friend of mine summed up his shipboard experience that makes sense in all leadership endeavors: Make a decision. If you're wrong, you'll know right away that it needs to be fixed. If you're right, things improve. If you don't decide, you've lost control and nothing can help.

Think about that with, say, your online fundraising strategies. There are so many ways to go that it can throw your team into analysis paralysis. How much thinking and debating and scrutiny need to occur before you say, "Go"? Don't agonize over your choices. Pick a viable approach and put it into play. With so many digital tools available for almost instant campaign feedback, you'll know almost right away if it's working and whether you need to make a course correction.

I know it's a bit disheartening to realize errors will always be in your future. However, if your nonprofit has a structure and culture that are built to adapt, your organization can take those missteps in stride and minimize their occurrence.

What does that mean, exactly? Simply put, don't share only the sunshine at board meetings or all-hands get-togethers. Communicate the misses with your team and supporters. Impart any lessons learned and how your group can overcome them. Encourage feedback, innovation, and collaboration. Ensure everyone knows that they're an important part of the process and that their efforts help move the organization forward.

Don't let other nonprofits set your pace or lead your way. As the saying goes, if you keep looking left and right (at your competition), you're less likely to move forward. This is not to say you shouldn't know what they're doing. After all, you're going for the same limited pot of donor dollars, and scouring other approaches can unearth those that align with your strategy.

However, be proactive and not reactive. Set your own standard and do what you think is right. Too often, organizations see their competitors doing something different and agonize over whether they're missing the boat by not following suit.

Grow the way and at the speed you want to. Be your nonprofit-self, let your North Star guide your decisions, and watch everything fall into place.

A GOOD EXAMPLE OF GOING YOUR OWN WAY

During one strategy and planning meeting, I was talking with the leadership team from a global humanitarian organization when someone suggested they needed to be canvassing—sending out teams to go door-to-door—because *Save the Children* (another super impactful organization doing profoundly important work) was canvassing. I asked why they believed this was the right move for them at the time, and the answer largely revolved around peer research results.

Canvassing can be hugely successful, don't get me wrong. But it requires ample resources, planning, training, and time to spin up. It didn't fit this organization's strategy and would've shoehorned them into doing something only for the sake of matching what someone else was doing. Worse, it would've detracted from efforts and resources needed elsewhere in their fundraising efforts.

On the flip side, this could've been an example of a big win—a successful fundraising campaign—if they chose to canvas.

In the end, they decided against it. Using brand integrity as a mini-North Star, they asked, "Do we want to be the organization that disrupts a commuter or customer's daily life on the street, even if that raises awareness and elicits funds from a select few?" The answer was "No."

Like I said, looking for ideas you can borrow as your own is never a bad thing. But don't for a second think you're behind because they did it first or that you're not as on-the-ball as they are. They got it from somewhere else, too, and who knows if it was the right move for them?

As opposed to the for-profit world, nonprofits are competitive yet ultimately rooting for each other. We're cheering for the causes and the communities we serve. We're in this together in some sort of charitable humankind dimension.

Nonetheless, the reality is that it's up to each nonprofit to survive and thrive on its own. That's an easier do for leaders who are decisive, make and share mistakes, and choose their own strategic path.

09

TO GET THERE, WE'LL NEED YOU, YOU, AND SOMEONE NEW

BOILING IT DOWN TO TWO

A leader's role when setting bold goals is establishing how to reach them. Most but not all of the time, that means aligning onboard talent and tasks to pursue firm priorities.

Conducting team evaluations allows you to optimize productivity. You can flush out capacity constraints and determine whether to fill operational gaps with in-house personnel or by hiring.

In an earlier chapter, I glossed over the all-too-common concern of capacity constraints—having plenty to do but not the team to do it—and said I'd get back to it. Well, here we are.

Actually, optimizing team capacity will be the underlying discussion over the next few chapters. The not-so-secret take-away? When status quo is the foe, leaders can reorganize their team to meet expanding needs.

You've put your growth mindset to work and established a bold growth plan. Perhaps it's a three-year target with hopes of, say, doubling your revenue—an energizing jolt of momentum toward your organization's vision.

Everything looks good; except your team appears to be maxed out in pursuit of only incremental growth.

Savvy leaders might ask how their team's size and skills line up with the newly established growth plan. They might quickly identify gaps, noting that the team, as it currently stands, appears insufficient for the tasks ahead. The solution may require hiring, but maybe not. So before they even think about crafting a clever job posting or two, they're going to evaluate their team against the top priorities.

I worked with leaders like this years ago and learned the genuine worth of prioritization. In a nutshell, efforts needed to accomplish management's priorities highlight staff strengths but also expose weaknesses. Only by knowing both can leaders craft a truly effective plan of action.

It was at a research-based nonprofit, one of my early jobs, where I first learned how efficient a team with set priorities could be. This nonprofit had a mission to improve learning for all kids through assessments that allow teachers to tailor education to the students. I found it to be really impactful work! Even so, the organization had been on cruise control for almost a decade with obvious lackluster growth.

So, the board hired a CEO who could shake things up. And shake 'em up he did! In my three years there, we rocketed from $70 million to $110 million in revenue. Among the ways we accomplished this was by aligning behind a clear list of priorities, which were passed down by the CEO, reinforced at every level, and translated into more granular priorities relevant to each department's function.

He also hired a Vice President of Sales with very specific skills. ("Sales" in this case referred to encouraging wider adoption of a teaching product rather than selling for a profit.) She turned out to be the most self-aware leader I'd worked for up to that point. Thanks to this new VP, I quickly learned the value of self-awareness in any role or position in a company.

By self-awareness, I mean an ability to perceive and understand the things that make you who you are as a person—the ability for you to get *you*. No easy task for any of us, since we're much more comfortable with the positive parts of ourselves (like strengths and talents). But I digress.

Our VP had the self-awareness to confidently state during her introduction that she had the skills to take us beyond $100 million in revenue, but not a billion. It was her sweet spot—where skills and experience align perfectly with the task at hand.

Admittedly, I don't think I could distinguish between abilities needed to reach $100 million in annual revenue versus those needed for a billion. If you searched online for billion-dollar skills (focus on what you do well, don't try to be what you're not, and so on), she seemed to have all of them. Nonetheless, she knew what she could do, and she did it by operationalizing the CEO's key priorities.

This was a big moment for the organization.

Why?

Because our CEO had hammered a big stake into the ground. He set a mammoth goal to support individualized education paths for three million children within the next three years. Not surprisingly, the programs we planned to expand to meet his vision demanded more revenue.

Accordingly, the CEO assessed our team against his goal, found a gap, and plugged it with the new VP. It was a great strategic call by a bold leader.

Our new VP then followed suit.

She evaluated the team's strengths and weaknesses to pinpoint gaps and make sure the team's roles and responsibilities were being utilized in the best way. To be completely honest, there were also people that had been around from the beginning who were quite resistant to change. (How do you think the VP handled them? How would you?)

> *Quick aside:* From my previous chapters, it's my hope that one of the key takeaways is viewing your people as your most valuable asset. Neither programs nor administrative functions run themselves, so put your hands together for your team. I'll also note that it's equally important for them to share in your desire to reach your benchmarks and put forth the effort to do so. After all, that's what *makes* it a team!

Conducting a strict assessment of your people's abilities can make all the difference between success and that other thing. A thorough assessment helps you (1) evaluate each person's talents (or lack thereof in some cases), (2) see who has the skills for the tasks ahead, and (3) refocus an individual's efforts based on strengths.

Let's say you want to start sending out a monthly newsletter, but you don't have a copywriter. After an ability assessment, you discover that—of the two talented people handling digital tasks like donor management and website upkeep—one of them also turns out to be a good writer. With some time and task realignment, your newsletter is a wrap without having to hire.

Later on, we'll delve a bit more into prioritization and what that means for every hour spent by every employee every day, including time off. After all, another benefit of surveying your team is finding capacity gaps in the first place.

The assessment of your team should also shine a light on the technology platforms with which they communicate, manage projects, create, and collaborate. Understanding the tools an organization uses is critical. It's an important part of evaluation and of your team's ability to take action on priorities. I'll talk about this in various forms throughout the book.

That's easy for you to say, Matt. But some of this is uncharted territory for me.

I know! And that's what I'm here for—helping you with these aspects and ultimately helping you improve and grow. I'll be covering more about such things later on. In fact, there's a step-by-step formula for employee evaluations coming up next.

10

AN INTERVIEW? BUT I ALREADY WORK HERE!

BOILING IT DOWN TO TWO

For any leader joining a new team or simply wanting to hit *reset* with an existing one, conducting "intentional discoveries" (i.e., interviews) with its members is a fantastic start for transformational growth.

Be sure to take thorough interview notes. Strategic questions can unearth enlightening answers, organizational blind spots, and adverse team-wide themes, making it possible to fix problems and optimize productivity.

No matter what you're driving toward, try to do so with a complete dossier.

Having a full picture of the situation automatically gives you a leg up as a leader. Whether you've recently been hired or promoted or you're setting a new course in a current position, gather every bit of information before making moves. To get specific here, I'm talking about learning what's going on from the perspectives of every individual on your team.

Good leaders should be the best listeners.

I help clients run what I call "intentional discoveries," and these listening sessions consistently prove to be illuminating for leadership teams. It's a simple but powerful process of interviewing your direct reports and below with purposeful questions meant to reveal more about processes than their performance—and by the way, that should be clear to them.

And it's not a bad idea to actually think of it as an interview.

I should also point out that through intentional discovery, you'll gain honest information of individual roles from their owners. This really does matter, because what people actually do shifts over time, and no one bothers to update job descriptions.

Whether it's a game-changing employee you've known for years or a staff member you're just now meeting, the steps and results involved with intentional discovery are about the same.

OUR CLIENT, A LARGE HUMANE SOCIETY: THREE THINGS THEIR NEW EXECUTIVE DISCOVERED

This well-established organization brought on a new senior executive ("the exec") to carry out an aggressive strategy, including introducing new services and expanding the physical campus to accommodate upcoming programs.

First things first. The exec astutely told us of a dilemma with the nonprofit's marketing and fundraising efforts, that they'd been operating with thin data and without a strong rationale. In short, they didn't know why they were doing what they were doing.

To me, it sounded like a "Because that's how we've always done it" situation. But there was only one way to find out.

I wasted no time directing leadership to set up individual interviews with everyone on the team. Next, I shared a list of questions that I'd been developing and updating over the years, meant to inform executives: *What's working, what's not, what's missing,* and *what's confusing.*

Typically, I'll insert personalized options as well, but feel free to bookmark this question starter-pack:

- Tell me about your role, responsibilities (and if a supervisor) the team you manage.
- What are your strengths and what do you see as the team's strengths?
- What are the challenges or pain points in your role?
- In your opinion, where are the organization's greatest opportunities for growth?
- What do you need or what needs to change in order to pursue these opportunities?
- Can you talk about processes and any systems you currently use; what's working and what's not?
- What do you view as priorities for our organization today and three years from now?
- What are the biggest barriers to mission growth?
- What if anything is being done to overcome those barriers?
- If you could make one change, what would it be?

Asking similar questions of their team, our humane society exec was hearing some consistent themes, and interestingly, I'd heard them before:

01. **Lack of clarity:** This existed at various levels regarding who makes decisions. As a group, it seemed that action items were agreed upon and yet often failed to get off the ground. Decision-making issues are more common than most people think and can have different root causes, but they're always an urgent problem. Luckily, as this organization found out, conducting an intentional discovery put them on track for a solution and clarity.

02. **Team at capacity:** This was no surprise, really. Even being at capacity, almost no one reported knowing where or even how to hit *pause*—in other words, everything was a priority. All said they were asked to do more and more, but not to stop doing anything.

    It's a common trait among team executors to crank on tasks and check boxes without thinking about why. They hadn't had a leader who could articulate the return on investment relevant to their roles or tasks or at all, and it was piling up. But things were about to change in that department.

03. **Confusion from working across too many systems:** We're at an innovative crossroads where new tools are constantly introduced. Sure, each on its own is designed to help humans work and communicate better, but it's a bit paradoxical because combining them tends to create confusion. There's

email, Google or Microsoft suites, texts, Slack, project management platforms, task management tools for developers, CRMs, and the list goes on.

Considering that conversations or comments are possible within each platform, it's not unheard of for people to get lost like this team did. Knowing that their work-tracking platforms had become more hindrance than help for most of the team gave the exec another area to improve, an area that could be a quick win simply by assigning communication rules and cutting power to nonessential tools.

The exec's discoveries were far from unique, making them a good example for other leaders like you. Our implemented solutions to these three pain points are conveniently in this book, so you don't have to look far—simply continue reading!

11

BAG THE LEADERSHIP VACUUM

BOILING IT DOWN TO TWO

Inviting your team to weigh in might take longer up front, but shared understanding and invaluable buy-in are worth the time.

Discuss with your team the challenges you've identified, create a smart plan together, and shepherd it with progress checks.

My team was hired to lead a collaborative planning initiative for an organization dedicated to ending poaching and illegal wildlife trading. We worked closely with an arriving Chief Marketing Officer (CMO) who had an impressive track record of building brand awareness. Importantly, she was also someone keenly aware of the impact an inclusive process can make. After landing on a strategy and operational plan, it would have been so easy, I would think *tempting*, for this leader to take it and simply tell her team what to do.

Nope.

Instead, the CMO brought it to her team for feedback, tweaks, and approval. Now, some may think this requires checking one's ego at the door, perhaps even demonstrates weakness, since it appears that she ceded power to subordinates. Absolutely not so! It's a leadership *strength*, because she was secure enough to let others weigh in and smart enough to actively listen to what they had to say. In the end, she knew she had the ultimate authority to decide and to act, so she yielded nothing. But what she got was the best strategy with everyone behind it from the start.

NOW OVER TO YOUR TEAM.

Coming fresh off the heels of an intentional discovery (see Chapter 10), look back at your notes and ensure you have an understanding of the challenges your nonprofit team is encountering. By the way, it's not a bad idea to run your observations and questions by your management peers. They may have run into similar situations.

Thorough evaluation of a problem is the first step in making any decision to overcome it, especially if you're new to the organization. Let the issue and its associated details sink in. Go for a walk. Take a drive. Sleep on it. The team is expecting to hear your marching orders—sooner rather than later—but at the risk of appearing slow to react, give yourself space to learn and form connections, to collect your thoughts.

You've heard from each team member their thoughts and feelings about whatever situation needs fixing. There's likely confusion, frustration, pressure, disappointment, maybe even apathy or some combination thereof on some level, or else there wouldn't be a problem.

During this contemplative break, you'll begin developing hypotheses about causes, effects, and possible solutions. They'll be invaluable as you invite your team into the conversation, because successful leaders-—like the CMO I discussed a few paragraphs ago—don't operate in a vacuum.

As noted earlier, the final call is yours to make, and you're in that role for a reason—to set the course.

Okay, so you know from your initial discovery that your team has ground-level insights, and now you too know what those are. So why is it so crucial to invite these people—your strategists, executors, builders, and maintainers who fill the ranks under your leadership—to also discuss direction? Isn't that your turf?

Of course it is. But like our CMO above knew, inviting their opinions creates vital *buy-in*.

A decision made behind closed doors can cause a team to feel shut out. Conversely, solutions discussed at a collaborative round table gives everyone a chance to share their perspective and to have a stake in the plan.

Start by bringing up what you've heard from them in your intentional discovery, and invite them into the planning process. Introduce them to a **problem-solving framework** to identify problems, solutions, and specific actions. After documenting and sharing your subsequent strategy, assign ownership by roles and responsibilities so everyone has a part to play.

BEING A MORE OPEN LEADER HELPED STEER AN IMPATIENT TEAM

We had another client, also a CMO, who felt pressure to move quickly to grow the organization. She found herself leading a suspicious team that had experienced three previous CMOs in four years.

I mean, yikes.

The team was at the end of its collective rope as far as trusting any new leader's vision. Their patience rapidly thinned as they waited for the now-fourth CMO to understand barriers to anything beyond incremental growth. However, shortcutting the time to know the organization—its challenges, its history, its opportunities—is not a step a good leader is likely to skip.

So we were brought on by this new CMO to help guide her and her team through in-depth discovery and strategic planning sessions. The team had every right to be frustrated initially. Who wouldn't be? However, once we explained our purpose and process, they were all onboard. The exercise proved worthwhile, and together, the team came out stronger on the other side. It didn't take long using our proven problem-solving framework.

A 90-DAY CHECK-IN

My final note on operating outside of a leadership vacuum is to re-evaluate at various points as long as it's needed. I suggest another round of one-on-one check-ins around 90 days into your plan's implementation. This iterative process will highlight what's working, what's not, what's confusing, and what's still missing.

You're a better decision maker when you have the necessary information, and you have a better chance of success with backing from your people. Note that having team support doesn't mean that everyone has to agree, and that's okay. You don't need unanimous consent, because **the tough decisions are yours to make no matter what**. But it sure is nice when people who share the same problem can also share in its solution. Never underestimate the power of buy-in!

Adopting such strategies should help your organization grow more quickly. But with growth comes change, and with change comes new, significant challenges.

12

CHECK YOUR SINGLE POINTS OF FAILURE AT THE DOOR

BOILING IT DOWN TO TWO

Anticipate and assess your team's single points of failure, and take action to provide backup where needed. This protects your nonprofit when a teammate performing critical tasks is gone or at capacity.

Eliminating single points of failure gives employees more space and focus to nourish those special projects your nonprofit needs to grow.

You're coaching a soccer team, and your only decent goal-keeper sprains an ankle. Now what? Sure, you'll throw someone in to plug the gap, but I think we can pin this one in the "Loss" column.

Introducing: *A single point of failure.*

Is just one person on your team capable of running a particular program? Can only one person launch and manage an email donor campaign? How about web maintenance, grant writing, payroll, and yes, even your responsibilities?

You could lose that special someone at any time through injury, illness, pregnancy, moving out-of-state, finding another job, caring for a loved one, and so on.

Or, a team member is suddenly overwhelmed with too much to handle from, say, a flood of incoming requests from high-level donors and corporate partners.

With no viable alternative or assistance for a critical position, your nonprofit is at the whim of luck and hope. And the more you grow, the more positions you have and thus the more susceptible you are to single points of failure.

This is not to say you'll avoid this entirely. In fact, it's a pretty safe bet you'll face it a number of times. After all, life happens to the best of us.

For *CauseMic*, I remember running headlong into single points of failure just after reaching $2 million in annual revenue. So we had to hire and hire fast if we wanted our own high-speed, integrated marketing team like those we help clients build.

But proper, deliberate planning can help minimize both occurrence and impact. This means anticipating the absence as well as the maximum capacity of your vital personnel.

You can prepare by either *hiring* or *cross training* multiple staff members for the same task. I learned a long time ago that, when doable, the best remedy is both.

I was leading an all-star fundraising crew at, you guessed it, *Team Rubicon*. And as I alluded to in Chapter One, this was when the organization was like the Wild West and moving so fast we were out of breath at the end of the day—or late into the night.

If you've been there, it's fun, right? An adrenaline-driven frenzy that makes it a fun challenge to wear multiple hats. But it's neither sustainable nor scalable, and it gets old quickly.

My team's players were skilled at their positions and—following our organization's beloved cultural principle—we were there to "get shit done." But I began to notice looming risks from single points of failure, and quite frankly, it scared me. So I did what any good leader would do: I decided to try something new.

I gathered everyone and began documenting what each person's *business as usual tasks (BAUs)* looked like over the course of a day, week, and month.

From a development and fundraising team, you might hear:

- Writing and sending donor acknowledgement letters
- Merging duplicate contact records in the database
- Updating donor information
- Cashing checks and logging donations
- Researching donor prospects
- Ensuring donor pipelines feature current cultivation, solicitation, and stewardship strategies

Great, you now have your list of business as usual tasks. The next step is to ask:

- Are there BAUs that we can discontinue?
- Who else on the team can do each BAU?
- Which teammates can be assigned as secondary and tertiary backups?
- Where and whom do we need to cross-train?
- Do we need to hire, be it full-time or contracted support?

I refer to this as establishing a team's BAU threshold. In other words, you're identifying capacity constraints.

I'm pretty sure it was a frustrating set of meetings, since I asked our team running full throttle to hit *pause* and explain what they do. However, when all was said and done, plugging single points of failure was the most important thing I did for our stretched-thin team.

Besides the obvious—not crashing and burning when someone leaves their post—your team will also have more time for special projects, meaning those that are NOT part of their typical task load.

ALLOW ME TO ILLUSTRATE WITH THIS EXAMPLE FROM A LARGE NONPROFIT (AND A PREVIOUS CLIENT):

This organization was spending way too long on their monthly close process. (For the non-accountants among us, *monthly close* is a series of steps and procedures that enable a company's monthly financial statements to be in compliance with the accrual method of accounting. It's done by for-profits and nonprofits alike.)

Anyway, their finance and accounting team was taking 17 days to do a monthly close. My first reaction was: *GASP! Seventeen days!* When I used to work in accounting at the nonprofit NWEA, we'd close in five days. But then I thought, maybe our speed was unique. As it turns out, most surveys indicate that more than half of organizations close in less than a week. So— *GASP! Seventeen days!*

Incompetence was not the issue. Rather, the team was constantly inundated by requests from other departments. Consequently, their work to close each month was frequently interrupted.

Our solution was to sit everyone down and review the six-person team's BAU tasks. In short, we helped them identify hiring and cross-training needs.

And here's the fun part: Over a relatively short period, they cut their monthly close down to fourteen, eleven, and finally four days! I'll let you do the math on how many individual hours were gained for special projects in a month—multiplied by the team's total number of employees. Never mind, I'll do it: 13 days saved = 104 hours × 6 people = 624 hours per month saved.

GASP! 624 hours that can now be used for special projects.

13

ASK YOURSELF: ARE HOURS REALLY OURS?

BOILING IT DOWN TO TWO

For capacity purposes, think like a for-profit. Use the adapted internal agency model to track time by projects or categories, and learn where your team is spending and missing valuable work hours.

To help grow your organization, use your utilization rate to guide your capacity decisions.

We all know *return on investment* (ROI), which basically asks whether the pay-off was worth the money spent. But what about return on time? (Let's not go with ROT). I'm talking about the hours spent by each team member during a workday.

Think about whether you actually know how each workday's hours are utilized at your organization. I'm not advocating a suspicious Big-Brother or eye-in-the-sky thing as if your people are slacking and can't be trusted. Not even close. I just want to share the huge advantages of tracking hours by project type using an ***adapted*** *internal agency model.*

What the heck is that?

In short, it's a type of structure that a service agency (like a consultancy, ad agency, or law firm) uses to distinguish billable hours (client work) from nonbillable hours (non-client work). I'm pretty sure you don't invoice your nonprofit's clients for your work, and so *billable hours* don't pertain. Thus the descriptor "adapted."

And believe me, this model is not too radical or too much or too complex for your group. Hear me out—especially if you're interested in ditching flat or moderate year-over-year growth for anexponential leap.

In essence, make every hour across departments count! Tracking hours like a for-profit agency is the only way to know where your team's capacity is stuck in the mud and where it has room to bloom. The smart play, then, is to use available capacity to the fullest to fuel your nonprofit's growth.

UTILIZED OR UNDER-UTILIZED? THAT IS THE QUESTION.

A for-profit's billable work hours are obviously its most valuable, because they produce company revenue. When compared to total hours on the books—i.e., billable plus nonbillable (admin staff, research, waiting for client input, management meetings, paid holidays, vacation, sick days, etc.)—we get a utilization rate expressed as a percentage.

(And yes, admin staff that is traditionally non-billable should be included. This helps leadership better understand if there's a good balance of billable versus nonbillable people on the team.)

For example, if an agency's work week consists of 900 hours billable to clients and a total of 1200 hours on the books, the utilization rate is 900/1200 = 75%.

As a note, industry standards suggest that a good utilization rate falls between 80 and 90 percent.

Okay. So, how do we adapt this to nonprofits? What replaces billable hours as the most crucial for a nonprofit?

I'd replace them with what I call "productive hours." As such, your utilization rate is:

Your team's *productive hours* divided by their *total hours on the books* (expressed as a percentage)

Ultimately, only you can determine what "productive hours" are for your nonprofit. But I can touch on some guidelines and perhaps suggestions.

Certainly, *productive hours* depend on your team members' roles. This means assigning importance to projects, functions, and programs to determine your number of productive hours.

For example, how many hours are they performing mission-related tasks, such as facilitating programs? How many hours are spent writing proposals or measuring outcomes as specified by grants? How many hours are spent on outreach, creating donor communications, or fundraising in general?

By specifying these as productive hours, you also shine a big light on everything else.

In addition to paid holidays, vacation, sick days, and the like, this may include your program facilitator's down time between preparing for that day's program and waiting for clients to arrive. These are *not* productive hours.

Also down time is that which your proposal writer waits for pertinent information from the funder. Or your digital campaign just launched, and now your team anxiously but idly awaits its results. These are *not* productive hours, either.

In addition to down-time hours, there are work hours that aren't in the "productive" category but are absolutely necessary, like, say, professional development or team happy hours.

SO—we now have productive hours and all the others. Easy enough to figure out your nonprofit's utilization rate, yes?

And what rate will you be happy with? You now know where unused capacity exists. You can increase your utilization rate by ensuring that capacity is filled with productive hours. That's something you can do right away to assist with your organization's growth!

Thinking about your team's utilization can be simplified by asking: Are we working on what's most important to our growth? For example, at *CauseMic*, we closely track non-billable hours by work categories such as, sales (Scale Sessions and proposals), marketing (speaking engagements, articles, paid ads, and this book), professional development (certifications and conferences), and paid time off.

What benefits derive from categorizing hours?

For me, I'm able to see what's moving the needle, where the team is focusing non-client efforts, and perhaps where we need to re-focus. What we've come to realize is that you're blindly steering the ship if you're not tracking hours this way.

Without question, the majority of our team's hours are dedicated to clients, but we can't forget to give our own mission a little love.

I didn't always have the headspace to focus on our own needs as a company.

I was averaging 63 hours a week—not uncommon for business owners. I just didn't have the time to even *think* about optimizing our own marketing strategy due to account management duties and administrative things like new employee onboarding. In short, it was not the best utilization of me as a leader.

Then, I hired a great executive assistant who could take my ideas, research curiosities, and administrative responsibilities and GO! It was amazing. I suddenly had space to think *"CauseMic growth."*

I rebalanced my own utilization as the company leader, and with my newfound mental capacity discovered that *CauseMic* could productize the services we offer to nonprofits. That was important to me. I wanted to make our expertise accessible at a lower threshold.

We've grown fast, because the demand for what we do is snowballing. Now, more nonprofit leadership teams are scaling their organizations using our *Rapid Growth Program*, a repeatable set of sprints proven to help nonprofits grow.

This book, for example, is an off-shoot of our *Rapid Growth Program*. Oh, and by the way, do you think I'd have time to write this had I not prioritized and focused on utilization? That's a hard "No."

THE CAPACITY TO HIRE

Using the adapted internal agency model will straight up tell you where you need to hire.

Here's a quick example: As it turns out, *CauseMic's* technology expertise and systems implementations—more on this in later chapters—were extremely sought after. In fact, our tech team members could not keep up with demand, as each averaged over 40 hours a week on billable implementations along with internal responsibilities.

Burnout is very real, and it's something I take very seriously. It seemed inevitable without intervention of some sort.

What we had was a *capacity constraint*, not a *capability constraint*. What *I* had was confidence to hire, thanks to the hours-tracking data. I could see how much time these concurrent projects were estimated to take and the number of capable teammates we had to operationalize them. So, we promoted one person and hired two new specialists.

One final note of caution unrelated to the example: A team member who is under-utilized and has *capacity* may not have the *skills* to fill a different role. As such, you could be wasting a lot of time and money assigning them with a certain task based on their available working hours. For instance, a data analyst might not be a great fit for donor relations.

Thus, temper your utilization discoveries with a realistic assessment of capability!

14

HIRE WHEN IT HURTS!

BOILING IT DOWN TO TWO

Maxed out capacity may be a sign of imminent growth—and burnout.

Take advantage of a growth moment by fearlessly hiring for the future—regardless of uncertainty.

If the title of this chapter doesn't give away my next recommendation, here it is: Hire when it hurts—when your team has been stretched to its fullest capacity.

I understand the resource constraints you're likely dealing with, because nearly every nonprofit will be tight on cash at various phases of growth. However, if everyone is starting to hurt and burnout is a legitimate concern, hire. Budget be damned, hire!

I give this advice with the utmost confidence. We've done it countless times at my firm, and continue to see the benefits of expanding our team and abilities in the process.

Brian, who runs strategy for a large consultancy, once gave me this advice when *CauseMic* seemed to be burning out. I had mentioned to him being unable to guarantee the longevity of our clients' work at the time, which began a fruitful conversation around optimization and utilization.

Think back to my earlier chapters where I talk about setting priorities and focusing the team's efforts across each role. As a leader, only AFTER you have (1) set clear priorities, (2) optimized employee utilization to achieve those priorities, and (3) confirmed that your team is in fact at capacity should you hire.

In spite of the uncertainty of future work, Brian and I agreed that hiring was called for when a truly forward-thinking company with a growth mindset was officially running on fumes. Even though that's when it hurts the most.

Because here's the thing: Your team might be at capacity and hanging on all right; but I'd bet they have little or no time at all to think about ways to improve processes and the organization as a whole. And that's especially important for moving through the phases of growth.

You also want to be prepared by having enough staff to say "Yes" when new opportunities emerge for your mission.

Realistically, especially for nonprofits, having a consistent operating cadence is hard to guarantee one way or the other. Needs of the communities you serve will ebb and flow, as will donations and other funding streams. So, embrace a growth mindset—and when it really starts to hurt, hire. That being said, if you *are* certain that the current work is for a limited time, consider hiring temporary contractors to fill gaps.

I've recommended to many clients to hire during pivotal moments in their growth phases, including at the onset of the pandemic.

While the world was shutting down, a small but mighty regional organization in Idaho was suddenly inundated with requests for assistance. The *Community Resource Center of Teton Valley* (CRCTV) provides help to families in dire financial circumstances and experienced aid applications at a daily rate higher than that of their typical month.

They reached out to us for help in handling the influx of applications, and we got to work for them immediately. In a four-day design sprint, we got them up and running on *Salesforce*, plus necessary integrations. And thinking ahead to building brand awareness with new donors, we launched a multichannel marketing campaign at the same time.

The best news is CRCTV was able to successfully catch up and disperse funds, providing needed relief to families hurt by the pandemic's economic distress.

Now, let's talk about recurring duties compared to time sensitive work (or a busy season).

In CRCTV's case, it seemed like a temporary spike in requests at first, and they didn't want to hire. I saw it differently. I saw how the rising requests could easily become steady recurring work, which would call for new streams of revenue to support it—greater needs equal more opportunities for services and more services require more donations.

In conversations with their Executive Director, I pointed out that they'd set a new bar for sustainable revenue and this was their new normal. They therefore needed to hire, even though it hurt to consider additional salaries so soon after being underwater.

This was an example of a wisely cautious leader who wanted to wait and see if the new systems we installed took care of the long hours. However, technology cannot fill every role. Rather, it's complementary to human leadership and ingenuity.

And while this organization's efficiency improved dramatically, their team, like so many, maintained an incremental growth mindset rather than one of exponential growth, which encourages *forecasting* for what's to come rather than *looking back* to determine hiring.

Ultimately, they did end up hiring, and they've continued to grow.

15

TELLING IT STRAIGHT

BOILING IT DOWN TO TWO

If an individual needs to be let go, be direct but compassionate; as hard as it is to fire someone, it's even harder to be on the receiving end.

Like any planned meeting, it helps to be prepared.

Firing or having hard conversations doesn't have to be a completely negative experience from either side of the desk.

Not when it's done with "compassionate directness," a phrase and practice coined and taught by Arianna Huffington, Founder and CEO of *Thrive*. She's also an author of many great books on this and other topics.

Obviously, since I'm using a phrase like "compassionate directness," I'm going to tell you to be nice. But, compassion involves deeper emotional thought and empathy than simply being polite and hoping the interaction is over quickly. You're entering into a conversation—two humans talking about the situation they're in—and neither particularly wants to be there.

This is where directness will be appreciated over vague reasons with an HR ring to them. Most people want to hear it straight. It can be hard to take, but it shows a level of respect that you are willing to say something that is more likely to initiate a conversation—especially a tough one.

Believing all you need is a line like "We've decided to move in another direction" leaves you unprepared and them incomplete.

It shows you're choosing to say something the *nice* way and hoping it does the job to avoid conversation or conflict. And sometimes it probably does just that.

At the end of the day, you know the outcome is the same and the conversation won't change your opinion. But it's for you to decide what you want your lasting feeling with them to be.

While I've had to fire a number of people in my career, one stands out in particular because it went well.

There had been previous cautionary conversations with this individual and an improvement plan for them to follow. Nonetheless, at a certain point, we no longer had time for this manager to grow into the role. I let them know that I valued their work ethic and talents in certain areas; but unfortunately, their talents and knowledge were lacking in the areas where they were needed most.

I was shocked at this person's reaction to my news. They were basically in agreement that they were not right for their role. It felt to me as if they needed to hear it to mentally move on to something else. It did in fact turn into a longer but good conversation, and it was an amicable split that taught me a valuable lesson. It served as a turning point for me—the new bar I set for myself when engaging in difficult conversations.

I got my proof point a few months later when I wrote a LinkedIn post on how to fire with compassion and directness, and that former employee positively acknowledged the post.

LESSONS FROM A CLIENT:

Right on the cusp of launching a year-end fundraising campaign, we heard from a longtime client that they would be firing a flaky strategist on their team. *Flaky* wasn't our adjective, but it was the right one. I'll admit I was relieved, because we'd seen the writing on the wall for some time and had told them this person wasn't delivering the way they should be. During a team workshop we led for their organization, we picked up on how others on the team were getting annoyed with this strategist's ineptitude. You could cut the tension in the room with a plastic butter knife.

The biggest obstacle for the organization's leaders was the timing being so close to year-end, when the majority of annual nonprofit donations are made. I understand how that can add fear, especially when your team is already at capacity. However, with the rest of the team picking up the slack or not having what they needed, the delay just isn't worth it. Besides, it's just not fair to others who are taking care of business.

Before they let this person go, they asked us for our perspective and advice. We said be compassionate and be direct. Explain that this individual had been allowing responsibilities within their role to fall through the cracks and it's hurting the team.

It was a large adhesive bandage to rip off, but it was unavoidable. All you can do as a leader is go about it with empathy in considering where that person is at, what they might've been up against, and telling them honestly why you have to part ways. This client made the tough call at a tough time, and their campaign was a success nonetheless.

Not that I think you don't already get it, but here are some steps I take in preparation for my own unavoidable conversations.

TIPS FOR PARTING WAYS WITH COMPASSION

- Gather the main concrete example(s) of underperformance that you used as rationale in making your decision. Refer to previous conversations you had with the individual.
- Be prepared to talk about the example issues in detail, but don't plan to unless asked—no need to squeeze a lemon onto the cut.
- Think about the situation from their point of view, and consider other factors that could have affected their performance. You're not looking for excuses, but rather learning so that you can show you understand the entire situation.
- Find a particular strength that they do have—good communicator, skilled in an adjacent area, etc.—because while you're pointing out how they've dropped the ball, they may have done other tasks well enough, too.
- Rehearse before the meeting.
- At a relevant point in this final meeting, say thank you for something they did bring to the team.
- Stay strong.

16

A GROWTH PLAN THAT BREAKS THE MOLD

BOILING IT DOWN TO TWO

A *Rapid Growth Plan* is a repeatable and structured process that turns your vision into achievable action.

It has three core components, each in an integral role: The One-Page Strategic Plan, the Project Backlog, and the KPI Tracker.

I'm going to come clean about something. Of all the recommendations I've shared up to this point, this is the true diamond in the rough, the service that brings more nonprofits to our door asking us to help grow their mission. It's called the *Rapid Growth Plan*. It's a no-nonsense title that lives up to its name. In this chapter and the next few, I'm going to define the three components of our *Rapid Growth Plan (RGP)* and explain how they work together.

In many ways, my philosophy for growing a nonprofit organization has gone against the grain for most of my career. Other schools of thought just seemed intentionally slow and cumbersome. They felt inefficient. I listened and learned but could never get on board. So I started thinking differently, and as I began to put my philosophy into practice, the results were validating. I felt I was on to something. Luckily, I was surrounded by colleagues at *Team Rubicon* who were willing to ride the same mold-breaking express.

Back then, it was mainly a hunch and definitely not called the RGP (or anything for that matter). But then I did some major tinkering, tested it out on real initiatives, and decided to share it. I wanted to help nonprofits grow in way less time than most were doing.

CauseMic was founded on this growth framework, albeit not yet a nice tidy bundle like I'm about to present to you.

The truth is, we're taught that Rome wasn't built in a day. You put in the long hours and years of hard work and you'll get there. Well I'm impatient, and some things can be done faster and, with the help of *CauseMic's* RGP, better.

For purposes of this discussion, we'll call *30,000 feet* the big picture (the overall vision for the organization and oversight of all the parts as a whole) and *10,000 feet* general operational awareness without being mired in detail.

Something many nonprofit leaders find challenging is making decisions below their 30,000-foot perspective. In certain phases of organizational growth, this is a fine perspective from which to be calling the shots—especially if lower echelons operate effectively with some level of autonomy. But your organization has to get there first. You do so with a clear growth plan and operational insight around the 10,000-foot level, where your staff can turn your direction into action.

Why is the lower altitude so important? In general, executives have to deal with numerous factors external to daily operations. Community partners, funding streams both current and potential, legal ramifications, public relations, and the like keep many leaders busy and too far above the actual workings to provide needed ground-level strategy.

So 10,000 feet ought to do it. It's high enough for overall control and grounded enough to be understood by (and more useful to) your executors, who most likely make up the majority of your staff.

Now, on to the three components of the *Rapid Growth Plan*:

COMPONENT 1:
THE ONE-PAGE STRATEGIC PLAN (OPSP)

The way organizations go about strategic planning is broken.

You can spend three to six months and north of $230,000 compiling research and developing an exhaustive strategic growth plan for your organization, wrap it up in a binder, and distribute it to the team who might read it one day when they have time.

The problem isn't necessarily the strategy; it's the staggering volume of information presented. Contents are based on way too many hours of low-impact research for the myriad strategizing from numerous and questionably productive meetings. At best, a strategic plan amassed in this way will lead to 3–5% incremental growth in revenue after months of work and spending.

Another issue with a strategic plan that takes months to create is that it usually sounds (and probably is) too lofty—too out-of-touch for most roles. This could be because it was written for the approval of a 30,000-foot executive team and it's simply not relevant for practical use. Moreover, the typical planning process has no standard way to capture ideas and make them immediately actionable.

Last, I've observed that the longer the plan and process, the less confident that the executive leadership team is about prioritization and decision-making. If you're comfortable during the strategic planning process, chances are, you're doing it incorrectly. Naturally, you will have to cut off possibilities and opportunities to allow for intentional focus, and that's not easy. I've seen leaders work so diligently to validate their plan, with the goal of ensuring everyone feels safe. If your goal is harmony and consensus, then great. If you're looking to grow in a big, bold way, this is wildly ineffective.

That being said, there is a better way: The one-page strategic plan, or OPSP.

At *CauseMic*, we guide leadership teams through an expedited process that leaves them with an understandable, focused, and actionable strategy on one sheet of paper.

The runway for launching an OPSP starts with real talk—getting to know where the organization has been, its challenges and strengths, and where it's going. And where its going depends on what comes next:

01. First, we define a time-bound **revenue goal** — we push for double at minimum—that's bold enough to stretch capacity without living in the clouds.

02. Next, the team will identify **the who** (or, audiences) which will likely include new target groups since this is a growth plan.

03. Once those are agreed upon, it's on to capturing the *what, when, where,* and *how*, which along with the who, constitute **your big five**.

04. Now you detail **your big five** and the opportunities identified for greatest impact. For example, ***what*** could mean program expansions or marketing the mission's programs to a wider audience, while the ***where*** might be focused on new geographic epicenters with larger opportunity. ***When*** equals moments throughout the year when a particular mission is more active based on need and attention. And ***how*** will include three to four strategic objectives that will guide your team to remain focused on the organization's strengths and opportunities. Examples include reaching a new audience, rolling out a new brand platform, investing in the infrastructure to reduce manual, repeatable processes, or leading with data.

05. Finally, **distill everything above down to one page**—hence the name One-Page Strategic Plan. It's deceptively simple but will challenge you and your team. It's not only possible but absolutely doable, or I wouldn't be writing this chapter.

COMPONENT 2:
THE PROJECT BACKLOG

From the process of creating your OPSP, your team will develop ideas on how to put it into action. And, by the way, that's the first sign that your OPSP is working.

As these ideas take shape, they will turn into projects. At first, they're floating around in the minds of your team, needing to mingle with previously known tasks so they can be assigned a priority hierarchy. We like to keep it simple and rank priorities as one through four. A priority 1—or P.1—is a top priority whereas a P.4 is in the lowest category. You may be tempted to add additional levels. Don't! Simplicity is key. Less is more. Make it easy for you and your team to prioritize what needs to be done.

I'll spell it out using a great example from our clients at *Thorn.*

Thorn had a list of things they wanted to accomplish, such as implementing a new customer relationship management (CRM) platform—a high-impact move for sure, but also one requiring significant cost in dollars and effort. Working with their team, we decided a new CRM platform was a lower priority—a P.2.

This is key, because they had a handful of other projects like routine website updates (improving donation pages, adding Apple Pay, etc.) that would make a big difference and not cost as much or require the same degree of effort. High-impact updates doable with low effort and low cost are always going to be top priority. So *Thorn* had quick wins queued up and ready to go, and those became their P.1s.

Since project ideas derived from your OPSP can't just float around and expect to get accomplished, they go into a *Project Backlog*. Any ol' Excel spreadsheet or Google Sheet will work, as long as it's organized.

For our clients, we build extensive Project Backlogs full of P.1s through P.4s. This is the visual aid we use to help define the impact and effort of each a project, which you first saw in Chapter Three.

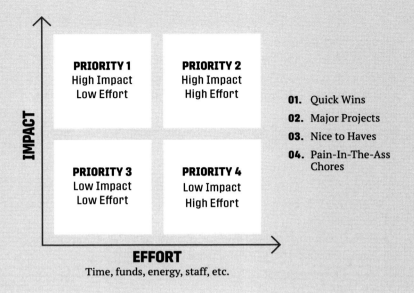

PRIORITY 1
High Impact
Low Effort

PRIORITY 2
High Impact
High Effort

PRIORITY 3
Low Impact
Low Effort

PRIORITY 4
Low Impact
High Effort

IMPACT

EFFORT
Time, funds, energy, staff, etc.

01. Quick Wins

02. Major Projects

03. Nice to Haves

04. Pain-In-The-Ass Chores

Load up your Project Backlog with all your hopes and dreams and score them accordingly.

As we all know in business and life, things can suddenly pop up that require immediate attention. Although they aren't officially prioritized, it's a good idea to add these to your Project Backlog and perhaps color them in red (or give them a priority label of P.Now).

It's good to include these pesky urgent needs for purposes of accountability, which is my final note on building your Project Backlog. Without accountability (responsible party, time frame, status, etc.), you're wasting your time having a backlog at all.

Put someone in charge of the Project Backlog who can manage and update it and keep the team accountable.

And note this: A P.4 in your Project Backlog does not deserve to keep getting bumped; eventually, it has to be promoted or removed.

COMPONENT 3:
KPI TRACKER

As a data-driven organization, you no doubt focus on *trailing (or lagging) indicators* to see what's happening, thus having a basis for, say, course correcting a fundraising campaign.

On the other hand, *leading indicators* are essentially predictors. Let's say joblessness in your metro area recently increased. This may be a leading indicator for you to at least prepare to augment your employment assistance program.

Without data, we're rudderless for sure. However, there's only so much data your team can wade through; plus, too much data can paralyze decision making. Thus, conserve your team's capacity (and your peace of mind) by latching onto only those numbers that matter the most for you: Your Key Performance Indicators, or KPIs.

For example, three leading KPIs that are universally important to nonprofits who are raising money online include:

01. **Website traffic:** How many visits your website receives
02. **Conversion rate:** How many visitors completed a donation
03. **Average gift amount:** Which may differ by campaign

Those are your big online fundraising indicators. They're a valuable starting point, but not the do-all-be-all by any means. In fact, for some organizations, dedicating too much effort to improving these fundraising data points might not be their best bet. Your OPSP should guide you in deciding what matters most to your organization.

Other important numbers to look at include indicators for grants, which demonstrated strong potential for the *Armed Services Arts Project* (ASAP) when their mass market revenue wasn't growing as steadily as they liked. Due to their investment in reporting on the effectiveness of their programming, the organization recognized a big strength: their grant application success rate. They also assessed the number of grant awards given out in their field, number of overall applicants, and percentages awarded.

Doubling down on grant applications enabled the team to focus on an alternative, and frankly larger, revenue stream to grow their mission. For organizations focused on grant funding, your KPIs might be:

01. Grant applications you submitted
02. Conversion rate: How many were awarded to you
03. Average grant amount awarded: How many grants are needed to fund your mission

The KPI Tracker is something we help teams create and manage as a finishing touch on their complete *Rapid Growth Plan*. And, like the OPSP and the Project Backlog, it's customized to meet their needs. Here's an example of how this might look for a nonprofit focused on growing online revenue.

KEY PERFORMANCE INDICATOR	ANNUAL GOAL	YEAR TO DATE	% TO GOAL
Website traffic (# of unique visitors)	500,000	170,000	34%
Online conversion rate	3%	3.75%	125%
Average online gift amount	$150	$145	96%
Online revenue	$2,250,000	$924,275	41%

If you have specific questions or you'd like more information about this three-component growth booster, just go to *causemic.com* and schedule a free Scale Session.

17

USE A FIRM STRUCTURE FOR SOLID DECISIONS

BOILING IT DOWN TO TWO

Consensus is useless when it comes to decisions; it lacks ownership and responsibility.

For deciding major issues, you'll want to give S.P.A.D.E. a chance. It enables buy-in without consensus.

Having experienced nonprofits both from within and as a consultant, there are two things that cause-driven organizations are generally proficient at: Conducting unproductive meetings and postponing decisions. Generally, the two go hand in hand.

Many nonprofits try to operate with consensus. If everyone agrees to this or that, then it's obviously a good decision, right? But if there is no consensus, "Let's think about it and reconvene next week to see if we can all come together on this."

Either way, nothing is likely to happen. That's obvious with the delay scenario. But even the situation in which there is consensus will flop for one distinct reason: There is no ownership.

I spoke earlier of how beneficial it is for a leader to get buy-in from the team. However, buy-in isn't consensus—buy-in is what you get when you listen to and consider everyone's opinions. Everyone has a voice, and that's what's important. But at the end of the day, the decision must be made by the right person who clearly communicates it and musters the team for action.

For rapid growth to occur in any organization, decisions must be made and done so in a timely, effective manner. Achieving this without consensus can be uncomfortable but is absolutely necessary to ensure ownership.

But now that we've established that, exactly who *does* own it? Who is the right person to make the decision (it's not always you)? Who approves it? When does it need to happen? These and other crucial bits of information are necessary to make and execute important decisions.

TO CAPTURE THAT INFORMATION EFFECTIVELY, YOU NEED A STRUCTURED FRAMEWORK.

For our clients and for ourselves at *CauseMic*, we use a system called S.P.A.D.E., which was developed by Gokul Rajaram while at Google and Facebook and first launched during his time at Square.

S.P.A.D.E. is a comprehensive process that's tailor-made for *important* or *tough topics,* like merging with another organization, creating a new department, overhauling technology, or changing the mission. If you want a decision on dark or medium roast in the break room, just get a hand count at happy hour.

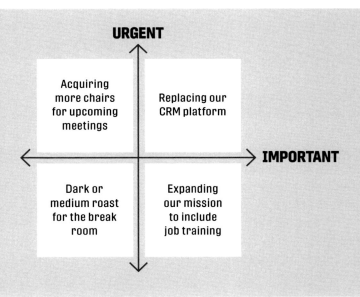

For each decision to be made, S.P.A.D.E. requires:

- **Setting**—This is the *what, why,* and *when* of the particular issue. For example:
  - We have to replace our existing CRM platform, because required customization has become too difficult or impossible.
  - We need to decide on a new platform by March 15, because that will give us time to procure it, install it, train on it, and migrate our data to it before we kick off our year-end giving campaign.
- **People**—These include the person responsible for making the decision, the approver of the decision, and those who are consulted for input.
- **Alternatives**—These are what your squad of consultants identifies as possible solutions that are *feasible, diverse,* and *comprehensive.*
- **Decide**—After you've laid out all possible alternatives with metrics like pros and cons, your consultants vote. Importantly, this should be private to squelch any influence arising from groupthink or leadership bias. After the vote, the decider decides.
- **Explain**—The decider lays out alternatives and the decision to the approver. Once approved:
  - The decision is explained in a commitment meeting to all consultants who are asked to agree or disagree publicly. This enhances their involvement and helps solidify their support.
  - The decision maker figures out next steps for delegation and execution.
  - The decision's S.P.A.D.E. is documented in a one-page, transparent synopsis and promulgated organization-wide for to all to see.

We've used S.P.A.D.E. with rousing success at organizations of all sizes. One that's recent to this book's writing stands out in particular.

GUIDING A GLOBAL ORGANIZATION WITH S.P.A.D.E.

CauseMic led a strategic planning meeting for an organization I'll call *Global*, which provides needed items to various world locales. *Global* had grown substantially with teams in numerous countries, ultimately forcing a crisis of control and a lack of mission clarity.

The problems facing *Global* were fairly numerous, but could be distilled down to three:

01. *Global* had amassed a lengthy list of challenges, which were boiling over to frustration at all levels.
02. The organization had *many* urgent decisions that had to be made, some that were endemic to specific locations.
03. The general vibe was one of optimism that solutions were within reach, but there was no lucid manner with which to nail them down.

To address these weighty issues, we were asked to facilitate a meeting abroad, attended by their senior leadership and the dozens of representatives across their many programs.

In a nutshell, we facilitated with S.P.A.D.E., and the results were outstanding.

We first elicited the list of decisions that needed to be made. They had never before been put in writing and listed on one form. The fact that 30 big decisions that needed to be made was our audience's first big eye-opener, with no less than this as the first one on the list:

What should our leadership structure look like?

I mean, wow. If that's not an important decision to make, I don't know what is. And without a framework like S.P.A.D.E. to guide them, it could be debated and unresolved until Apple makes its final iPhone version. And who's got that kind of time?

Subsequently, we asked each person in the room to answer four questions:

01. What two to three organizational decisions should take top priority and why?
02. Who should be the decider of each?
03. Who should be the approver of each?
04. By what date should these decisions be made and why?

With answers in hand, the list of 30 issues was reorganized by priority, and *Global* ended the meeting knowing who was going to decide what, by when, and from whom each decider should seek approval.

As a note, the information was documented in a "Global S.P.A.D.E. Backlog" Google sheet, with progress updatable in real time by all applicable players, regardless of location.

Using S.P.A.D.E., we helped *Global* replace chaos with order and prepared them for their next phase of growth.

If only we'd had it years earlier for another global group, as you'll soon see.

18

IDEAS ARE SHIT WITHOUT EXECUTION

BOILING IT DOWN TO TWO

A good plan means little without proper execution, and vice versa.

Using the right structured frameworks, both can occur for exponential growth.

In the previous chapter, we discussed how S.P.A.D.E. is invaluable for assigning ownership to each major decision. Knowing who is responsible, who can approve it, and when it should be executed is a huge part of the puzzle when it comes to growth initiatives.

I'd have to say this is a very big deal. Because no matter what you want to accomplish, **it's just pie-in-the-sky unless you execute your plan**. I believe the chapter title nicely sums up my feelings about this.

After initial execution, you'll want to track progress and discover any previously unseen roadblocks or challenges. Quickly determine your course corrections, and execute them as well.

By the same token, if you don't have a good plan or the right plan, then executing it is an exercise in futility. This is especially true when it comes to your strategic plan. To us at *CauseMic*, the latter should be one of exponential rather than incremental growth. I'm talking about matters like doubling your revenue within three years.

And as good as S.P.A.D.E. is, it's not a method for creating such a plan. Accordingly, I want to touch on *CauseMic's Rapid Growth Workshop (RGW)*.

Our *RGW* consists of just four half-day sessions spread over three weeks. Each of these mini-workshops consists of structured exercises designed to elicit honest, essential, and comprehensive information from your team.

Upon RGW's completion, you'll have a one-page strategic plan (that's right—one page!) for your organization. A winning, no-fluff, inclusive, action-oriented plan.

At the very top is your purpose statement, followed by the goals, challenges, and recommended actionable steps determined during the four half-day workshops. And all details from the *RGW* are captured in a shareable executive summary for your easy future reference (so notetaking isn't even necessary!).

Just think—You can use the *Rapid Growth Workshop* for developing all of the *whats* and *hows* your nonprofit needs for exponential growth. And use S.P.A.D.E. for assigning the *whos* and *whens*.

That's a pretty potent combination of frameworks—and we can facilitate both for you!

They're good examples of three of *CauseMic's* cultural principles:

01. **The future belongs to the curious:** We're always looking for new ways to help our nonprofit clients become fully funded. That's how we came across S.P.A.D.E. in the first place.

02. **Sleeves up:** When we find something that has potential, we work to adapt and optimize it to meet the needs of each specific client.

03. **Success is not final:** Just because something works doesn't mean that it can't work even better. Just think how *RGW* and S.P.A.D.E. can complement each other.

Speaking of S.P.A.D.E., I wish we would have had it years ago for a fundraising program spawned by a global humanitarian agency.

This was to be a coordinated campaign, an essential aspect since it involved numerous member countries along with multiple marketing agencies and governmental entities.

As you can imagine, more than a few challenges arose involving differing views, conflicts of control, languages, objectives, plans, and ways to track program effectiveness.

No one really knew whose decision anything was, who would approve it, and when it should be put into play. In short, it was a huge effort by lots of players that translated into a big waste of time with very little impact. For example, the goal for the

U.S. pilot program was less than $30,000. And the only reason why the program achieved that goal was because one individual donated more than half of the amount. But as small as that U.S. fundraising pilot program was, it took over 600 staff hours about 40 pages to document its after-action summary.

Yikes!

We knew then that we needed a framework we could put into play should we ever again be in a similar situation. That's when we found S.P.A.D.E. and realized how valuable it could be for executing major decisions in nonprofits both large and small.

Because without execution, ideas are—well, you know.

19

MAYBE YOU DON'T KNOW YOUR OWN STRENGTH!

BOILING IT DOWN TO TWO

Discover that one fundraising superpower: Is it storytelling? Partnering? Is it your voice? Shepherding supporters? Accessing news outlets? Featuring a celebrity?

Once you know it: Harness it, improve it, leverage it!

I can't tell you how many times I've heard something like: "Well, they can raise more money because they help puppies, and people love puppies," or "They respond to natural disasters and have all that attention on people who need help."

Yes, puppies and disasters are noteworthy, but they're not strengths. They're just part of the mission. Strengths are how those nonprofits get across what they do regarding puppies and disasters that bring in the donations.

Every mission has a bigger audience of supporters out there that can be reached by taking advantage of its primary built-in strength.

I very much enjoy helping nonprofits discover their own superpowers in attracting more eyes and hearts to their cause. Sometimes they're obvious, but lots of times they're not.

It's a little like this personal strengths test I've done with my teams called the *Clifton Strengths Assessment*. It's a fairly well-known tool designed to give you a leg up in your career by identifying what you're best at, enabling you to work at developing that skill even further.

Of course, this runs contrary to many of us wanting to fix a weakness first. However, a widely accepted school of thought notes that focusing on your strengths can be more beneficial. It's one of those things we just don't instinctively consider when we think of "improvements." The same goes for marketing and fundraising.

Find what your organization does or can do well or where a particular opportunity exists, and squeeze every last drop of potential out of it.

For example, *Team Rubicon* has a distinct brand voice. Its military veteran-led mission of disaster relief and mantras like "We help people on their worst day" lend what many call a *gritty* voice to a noble image. We recognized this as a strength that could be leveraged to form partnerships with corporations having somewhat gritty reps themselves. It's no wonder, then, that meat-snacks giant *Jack Links* and workwear leader *Carhartt* joined forces with *Team Rubicon* to assist in its efforts.

I can't know your nonprofit's true strengths (yet!). Perhaps you do, yes? Nonetheless, I'll leave you with a few examples from these current or previous clients that may inspire your thinking.

CELEBRITY FORTUNE: THORN

Thorn is an organization that aims to eliminate child sexual abuse from the internet. It was co-founded by Ashton Kutcher and Demi Moore, so you can probably guess one of its strengths. Having a celebrity ambassador is a rarity for sure. A lot of organizations will devote (waste) time trying to secure a big name to back their mission. If you've got someone famous connected to your mission in some way, by all means go for it; otherwise, look to other superpowers.

Having Ashton to speak on behalf of their urgent mission helps bring mass market awareness and high-level donations on top of his own contributions. That being said, relying on a public figure comes with its own strings and stipulations, such as limited availability, supporter loyalty to the celebrity (not the nonprofit), and repercussions from any of the celebrity's public missteps.

STRENGTH IN NUMBERS: OPERATION GRATITUDE

Operation Gratitude wisely called upon its active volunteer base and raised $820,000 in one month. They did so via their partnership with *Jersey Mike's* of Southern California through its Month of Giving campaign in which a percentage of the proceeds from sandwich sales went to the cause. Basically, *Operation Gratitude* asked volunteers (who regularly team up at their SoCal warehouse to fill care packages for deployed troops) to also order their sandwiches from *Jersey Mike's* and spread the word.

Volunteer activation gave *Operation Gratitude* the edge and at virtually no cost. They reached volunteers via email and organic social posts. I'd say this could also be an example of thinking smarter not harder. Plus, ya know … partnerships!

LOCAL MEDIA MOMENTS: NORTHWEST MOTHERS MILK BANK

This was the case of an organization taking advantage of a timely opportunity to drive mission awareness and make a difference for their cause amid heightened need.

The nationwide baby formula shortage in 2022 verged on becoming a full-blown crisis for mothers and babies, drawing significant media attention. During the shortage, *Northwest Mothers Milk Bank* received an influx of calls from nursing mothers wanting to donate milk, and the organization was eager to do more. Accordingly, we advised them on how to get in touch with local news outlets. We saw that they had more opportunity seeking local versus national news coverage, because they operate locally, a sizable need existed in the region, and people are more likely to support locally in general.

Focusing close to home strengthened their resources and overall impact where it was greatly needed. Had they chosen to wade into national waters, their message may never have gotten through or could have been swallowed by similar missions, thereby missing out on a wealth of potential right around the corner.

STORYTELLING: DIGDEEP

DigDeep is a long-time client of ours, and they have a super-power that only seems to get stronger and more effective every year: Storytelling.

In the years we've worked together, we've watched their impact as well as donor engagement grow, due in large part to the quality of the content they share (particularly video). Moreover, donors are especially receptive to their first-person narrative style of storytelling, courtesy of a *DigDeep* staff member. Bringing supporters on a journey, she candidly shares her experiences of growing up in the Navajo Nation without running water. It's authentic, and it builds trust in the mission to bring clean running water to every American.

Another way they use their strength to its fullest is by segmenting audiences with whom they've previously engaged. These folks were privy to *DigDeep's* impactful stories regarding water projects in their locations, and DigDeep ensures they are the first to hear new ones.

Time and time again, *DigDeep's* storytelling has anchored successful fundraising efforts.

What it really comes down to is thinking creatively about what your mission is, how you do it, and whom it serves—because somewhere in there is your organization's fundraising strengths just aching to be unleashed!

20

DON'T MISS GOOD FOR GREAT!

BOILING IT DOWN TO TWO

Often, it's not only okay but much better to say, "This project is good enough," because it really is—now on to the next.

Perfection is the natural enemy of progress.

In an earlier chapter, I talked about how the real secret for growth isn't how perfect you are, but rather how *decisive* you are.

In the same vein, nothing impedes progress like passing up *feeling confident* for *being sure*.

Think of this in the context of submitting a grant proposal. Are you absolutely positive you'll be awarded the grant? Of course not. The best you can do is feel confident that (1) your North Star correctly guided you to the opportunity; (2) your proposal is well-written; and (3) you can effectively perform the services and reporting required by the grant should you win it.

You can use a similar view for other projects requiring a decision. When's the last time you *knew* that, say, sending another digital touchpoint in a fundraising campaign would definitely increase donations? Or that hiring someone to eliminate a single point of failure in your organization would be a successful hire?

The answer, of course, is *never*. But if you agonize over every decision, laboring to craft a fine edge and poring over the 360 degrees of potential consequences, you'll end up not just impeding progress but quite possibly falling even further behind.

Lots of time will have been spent before saying "Go" or "No" that could have been used for other things (now backlogged) requiring your attention. Not to mention that after a while, opportunities are no longer so if not acted upon quickly, like, say fundraising to help *current* disaster victims.

Take this book, for example. Did I perform weeks of market research to learn about the demand for a book like this? Was I certain it would be worth my time to write it? Not a chance.

No, I just knew I wanted to write this book, because its lessons have been valuable for our clients. I went with my gut feeling that it could thus be useful for nonprofit leaders. And that was enough for me to proceed.

Sure, it might have less than the anticipated splash. But at least I didn't waste my or my team's time researching an answer until we were blue in the face, only to tell us: *Maybe*.

At *CauseMic*, we work on a lot of websites, and of course we want the overall look, the copy, the function, the design, everything to be outstanding. However, early on we struggled to balance time and effort with a product we considered perfect and thus "finished." Clients were sometimes quicker to approve than we were.

What we learned is that (1) nothing is ever finished, and (2) getting the website out into the world to start doing its job was worth more than making minute changes for an extra week or so. We balance *excellence* and *functionality*, keeping in mind there will be upcoming iterations from real world feedback and performance regardless.

I'm not saying you should half-ass anything—I believe in the maxim, "If it's worth doing, it's worth doing well." But in the nonprofit world, time is *donations*. A campaign, website, or new program stuck on the launch pad has a 100% chance of going nowhere and doing nothing for your nonprofit. Whereas, any of those sent out into the world with *reasonable certainty* that they're good enough have a chance to succeed.

Don't let your organization become paralyzed by perfection.

You don't need a Strengths-Weakness-Opportunities-Threats (SWOT) analysis for every business decision. I do understand the need for research that supports, say, everything-is-on-the-line decisions. Merging with another nonprofit, changing or significantly expanding your mission, fielding multiple program locations—these require something other than a gut feeling.

However, I'm guessing the bulk of your decisions are somewhat south of life-changing events. As such, don't waste time and money on formally determining what your experienced gut feels is right. Remember what my naval officer friend said of decisions: "If you're wrong, you'll know right away that it needs to be fixed. If you're right, things improve."

Will sending that email late because you want to revise one sentence (kicking off another round of approvals) really bring in more gifts to make it worth it? Probably not. Hitting inboxes later might even hurt performance.

To start rapidly growing your nonprofit, practice saying, "That's good enough."

"That's good enough. Let's go!"

"That's good enough. Send it."

"That's good enough. Launch the program."

Okay. That's good enough. Let's go to the next chapter.

21

"THE HUMAN SPIRIT MUST PREVAIL OVER TECHNOLOGY"

— ALBERT EINSTEIN

BOILING IT DOWN TO TWO

You need technology, and technology needs control.

Invest in a team that ensures technology serves and grows with you.

You've made it to the final few chapters! Hopefully you've spotted at least a few valuable tips and new ways of thinking about your nonprofit's growth trajectory. And while I've alluded to technology throughout the book, it deserves a little deeper dive in its own space. So here we go.

Platforms, applications, and interconnected systems (your technical stack, or *tech stack*) are tools that comprise your nonprofit's internal command center. (If you don't have a tech stack, how come?)

It's through this command center that all operations are handled, be it fundraising, communications, donor management, administration, and what have you. And the bigger you get, the more unwieldy it can become—unless you have a technology team.

These are the folks dedicated to defining processes, to managing, implementing, and governing the technology. If something goes wrong, they can debug it. If a new need arises, they can create a space for it. If a current component is inadequate, they can upgrade or replace it.

Is it absolutely necessary for a new organization to have such a team during its initial phases of growth? Probably not. But then again, I wouldn't wait too long.

Take this not-so-hypothetical scenario, for example. The organization has a programs or operations team that needs to chat with volunteers across the world, so they might implement *WhatsApp*. The fundraising team is having conversations in *Salesforce*. The marketing team is collaborating on *Slack*, except its project managers who are commenting on tasks in *Asana*. The executive director has embraced *email* and email alone. Others are using *Google docs*. Where and how collaboration occurs is anyone's guess.

Now, if the team remains largely unchanged, they get used to this growing spider web of systems—like the proverbial frog in slowly boiling water. So it might actually work for a hot minute or two.

However, it *will* become a problem, especially for cross-team collaboration, as the organization expands in size and complexity and new people join. In short, the organization will lose control of its own command center.

That is, unless you put someone in charge of it as the start of your tech team. Just as soon as you can. You'll find it to be not only a great investment for your nonprofit's growth, but an indispensable one.

Along the way, you'll discover that not just any technology will do. Not by a long shot.

22

HMM...THE FERRARI OR THE KIA?

BOILING IT DOWN TO TWO

Overbuying your technology stack can be just as inefficient as underbuying.

Take the time to carefully consider your needs, and resist any pressure to make a quick purchase.

A proper digital transformation is crucial for nonprofit growth. Besides performing typical housekeeping tasks like accounting, a tech stack must accurately and efficiently handle the typical nonprofit's lifeblood: Donations. This involves a practical if not somewhat delicate balance between data requirements, cost, desired growth, and technology. Otherwise, bad things can and will happen.

On one hand—

Overbuying tech tools and platforms can mean a significant drain on a nonprofit's resources. It can also create a complex, inefficient, and confusing technology environment.

So why would anyone overbuy on purpose?

Well, one reason is having an obsession for acquiring the latest and greatest tools, even if they're overkill, with the mistaken belief that maximum capability equals maximum usability.

Overbuying can also stem from a lack of understanding a nonprofit's needs and the capabilities of its existing tools.

And let's not rule out the pressure to make quick decisions in a fast-paced environment. Nonprofits may feel the need to act quickly to keep up with the competition or, say, an increasingly larger influx of donors. As such, they may end up overbuying without thoroughly evaluating the potential value and impact.

But arguably the most common reason why nonprofits overbuy is overselling by tech vendors. Their job is to push the most expensive products, whether or not they reflect a realistic solution.

In the end, overbuying can mean:

- Higher costs of purchase and maintenance
- Increased complexity requiring more task time and training
- Snags from integrating new and existing tools
- Confusion and inefficiencies arising from a lack of familiarity

On the other hand—

Underbuying has its own set of problems. For one thing, an outdated tech stack may be unable to handle increased traffic, leading to slower performance and maybe even crashes.

A limited tech stack may not have enough features required for the nonprofit, ultimately hampering growth. And integrating new tools with it may not only prove difficult, but could cause compatibility issues.

SO—GET JUST ENOUGH TECH

It all comes down to understanding your organization's digital needs. Things to consider include:

- Website looks, functionality, hosting, and content maintenance
- Communicating with donors, subscribers, and volunteers
- Internal communications
- Storing, tracking, and using donor data
- Measuring and reporting outcomes of programs and services
- Human resources and finance
- Ease of tech component integration
- Cost (including purchase, maintenance, and training)

Some platforms provide lots of bells and whistles, many of which only the largest nonprofits need or can afford. Other platforms are more suitable for most nonprofits, offering desired upgrades that may or may not be worth the cost.

Let's use a Ferrari-versus-Kia analogy. **In this case, *the Salesforce Marketing Cloud is the Ferrari.***

As of this book printing, Ferrari models range from $2.25 million to a mere $222,000.

The highest price gives you 828 hp, while the "economy" version still provides 612 hp. How much power are you looking for?

Considering that most cars average 180 to 200 hp, any Ferrari model is more than triple the power that most folks need.

Plus, where the heck are you going? Most of us putter to places like the office, Costco, or a local restaurant, not rocket out to meet up with celebrities in the Hollywood Hills.

On the other hand, Kia models range from the $20,000 Soul to the $50,000 Sorento Plug-In Hybrid. **Let's call Kia the *Hubspot* CRM, which may be more in line with your needs.**

You just have to determine which model will work for you.

For example, let's say you need the Kia Soul with Smart Cruise Control. But the only model you can get with Smart Cruise Control is the Sorento. Do you really want to pay another $30,000 just to get that one feature, or will an available Soul with standard cruise control be sufficient?

○ ○ ○

The bottom line is, carefully consider your digital requirements, and resist the pressure to make a quick decision. You don't want to overbuy for the reasons noted earlier. But keep in mind that underbuying may hinder future growth and prevent effective integration with needed upgrades.

Lastly, you'll want a system that enables efficient data maintenance. This means things like duplicate donor detection and cleanup, merging donor information, or segmenting donor audiences based on personas (e.g., age, interests and concerns, donation frequency and amounts, locations, etc.).

CauseMic has a ton of experience matching tech stacks with organizational needs. I'm happy to discuss this with you—just go to *causemic.com* and schedule a free Scale Session with me.

23

MOVE SLOW TO MOVE FAST

BOILING IT DOWN TO TWO

Include a feasible discovery period in your plan to acquire the right technology, and especially consult with those who will be using it.

Don't let adoption be the forgotten child.

We just talked a lot about the importance of matching your tech stack to your nonprofit's needs. But how do you know which features you *require* as opposed to which are *nice to have*?

With thoughtful discovery.

Before you panic at the thought of endless interviews, know this; a discovery process need not take months. As noted in many of my recommendations, speed is just as important as substance. That said, an investment in time upfront will save you loads of cash down the road.

When I was at *Team Rubicon*, selecting our first CRM for fundraising was done in haste. Having never been through an implementation, I hired a consulting firm to assist. The hour-long call with their business analyst ended with him telling me exactly what technology we required and how much an implementation would cost. I've since learned their approach is all too common and way too wrong.

It turns out, **they didn't know much about our requirements and I didn't know how big of a problem that would turn out to be.**

So, what should they have done differently? They should have met with each end user to understand their goals and current pain points. They should have captured requirements as user stories and had us each identify *"must haves"* and *"nice to haves."* They should have taken those requirements and recommended more than one platform to demo for us. They should have documented our platform decisions with a future systems map and built an implementation plan that accounted for our unique needs.

Instead of technology making our jobs easier, we implemented a tech stack that did not meet our basic requirements. We thought we were ordering a sandwich, but ended up with unwanted soup and salad. **It was an expensive lesson that**

ultimately shaped how *CauseMic* approaches digital transformations.

Instead of meeting with an inexperienced salesperson, we have clients meet with a nonprofit technology specialist. They actually *consult*, which means they ask lots of questions and guide you toward a practical decision. They balance speed with quality— they know that moving too quickly during discovery will only cost you more in the long run, but that efficient discovery can minimize time involved.

Just like discovery, a plan for user adoption is more important than the build sprints themselves. Adoption is often the forgotten child. I get it. You want to be done once your historical data has been migrated from *Blackbaud* (sorry, not sorry) to *Salesforce* or *Hubspot*. A digital transformation requires end users to understand how the new system will improve their day-to-day work.

More often than not, technology consultants will put together training plans. These are typically incomplete. They don't cover the changes as to how people should work. For instance, they don't call out the need to develop journeys by audience (monthly donors versus major donors) and interest areas (plastic pollution versus clean water) and how this will impact the marketing team's capacity. They don't address changes as to how you should run your planning meetings, now that you can identify what content is performing best by channel.

A digital transformation done well will unlock exponential growth in revenue and impact. Done poorly, it will cost you time and money and set your nonprofit back.

So when considering a shift, be sure to set aside time to plan for both implementation and adoption.

24

LET'S GROW YOUR NONPROFIT'S REVENUE AND IMPACT!

And there you have it.

First and foremost, thank you for taking the time to read THE HIGH-GROWTH NONPROFIT: *Proven Steps to Quickly Double Your Revenue and Drive Impact.*

You've now gotten a lot of the truths and insights about running a nonprofit with a growth mindset, nuggets I've accumulated throughout my career from failures and successes alike.

If nothing else, I hope you've come away with the confidence to grow your mission as fast as possible. The world needs you to scale!

Certainly, no two causes are the same, nor are two nonprofits. So we can't paint all paths to success with the same broad brush. But as long as you set forth with a high-growth mindset and let your unique North Star guide you, your mission has every chance of changing the world.

My team and I are here to help you grow. I offer each leader a Scale Session—**a FREE NO-BS strategy call**—and regularly share tips through our newsletter, *Switchboard.* You can sign up for both at *causemic.com.*

If you know a nonprofit leader who would find the lessons in this book beneficial, please refer them to *causemic.com/givebook.* Both the book and shipping are on me!

In service,
Matt

ABOUT THE AUTHOR

Matt Scott is a nonprofit growth consultant and social entrepreneur. He leads *CauseMic*, a consulting firm specializing in helping mission-driven organizations like *Partners in Health*, *Greater Good Charities*, and *Surfrider Foundation* quickly grow revenue and impact. Prior to *CauseMic*, he led development operations at *Team Rubicon*, a disaster relief organization whose annual revenue scaled from $275K to $51M during his tenure. Matt is a sought-after speaker, sharing his approach to leadership and social impact at conferences like *Dreamforce*, *Twilio Signal*, and the *Nonprofit Technology Conference*. His commitment to doing business for good has been recognized with the Civil Service Award, the Arete Service Award, and the Riordan Service Award. You can reach him or subscribe to *CauseMic's* newsletter *Switchboard* at **causemic.com**.

ACKNOWLEDGEMENTS

To my partner, Jenna: Thank you for always allowing me to get to "Yes!" no matter how many hours I spend toiling away in my office.

Thank you to Paddy, Craig, and Drew for catching the little and big things on way too short of a turnaround.

Franny, thanks for helping us meet deadlines, spot risks, and identify dependencies.

Thank you to Chris for designing and laying out the book.

Thanks for allowing me to *step into the arena,* Jake. Grey-shirts always!

A special thanks to Bobbi—so much would be only an idea without you.

Most importantly, thanks to our clients, who trust us to take bold, calculated risks together.